Kerygma and Church

Interpreting Amos for Preaching and Teaching

Edited by Cecil P. Staton, Jr.

Smyth & Helwys Publishing, Inc.®
Macon, Georgia

ISBN 1-57312-026-X

Interpreting Amos for Preaching and Teaching
edited by Cecil P. Staton, Jr.

Copyright © 1995
Smyth & Helwys Publishing, Inc.®
6316 Peake Road
Macon, Georgia 31210-3960
1-800-568-1248

Library of Congress Cataloging-in-Publication Data

Interpreting Amos for preaching and teaching/
edited by Cecil P. Staton, Jr.
pp. viii + 168   6" x 9" (15 x 23 cm.)
(Kerygma and church)
Includes bibliographical references.
ISBN 1-57312-026-X (alk. paper)
1. Bible. O.T. Amos—Criticism, interpretation, etc.
2. Bible. O.T. Amos—Sermons.
3. Sermons, American.
I. Staton, Cecil P. II. Series.
BS1585.2.I57   1995
224'.806—dc20
                                        95-42100
                                          CIP

Contents

Preface to the Series

Smyth and Helwys Publishing presents the *Kerygma and Church* series in the hope of filling a void in literature available to ministers and churches. In particular, the series seeks to bridge the gulf too often separating the study from the pew and the academic classroom from the context of church life. The series legitimates its existence by the conviction that biblical scholarship has significant and relevant contributions to make to the ongoing life of the community of faith.

Because of its stated aim to connect the serious study of the Bible with the life of the church, the series intends to feature the contributions of persons who themselves are sensitive to the relationship between scholarship and church life. Whether the approach be primarily exegetical or expository, a sensitivity to both endeavors should be evident.

Both academicians and ministers/church leaders will find an avenue here to articulate their understandings of the Kerygma (the church's proclamation). The series further aims to be inclusive of the diversity within the total body of believers. While the series is expressly by Baptists and primarily for Baptists, an inclusive spirit will also at times lead us to consider other perspectives.

As students of Baptist history would expect from any endeavor invoking the revered names of (John) Smyth and (Thomas) Helwys, freedom of inquiry and expression is paramount for this series. A respect for scripture as authoritative religious literature bearing the Kerygma of the Word of God directs scholarship to listen carefully to what is said in order to learn how to respond faithfully. Beyond this healthy concern to "hear and obey," however, no other parameters are permitted to dictate the direction of study or the application of its findings. Through exegesis and exposition of biblical texts, the works of this series will strive to connect the Kerygma of God with the Church of God.

The Editors
Macon, Georgia

Editor's Preface

The publication of this volume and the companion student study guide by Robert G. Baker marks the sixth year Smyth & Helwys has provided resources for the midwinter Bible study conducted annually by hundreds of churches across the country. With these volumes we continue our commitment to provide quality resources that encourage the church in its pursuit of serious study of the sacred scriptures.

If this volume accomplishes its mission, you will find here articles, commentaries, and sermons that are valuable aids for teaching and preaching the intriguing texts of the book of Amos. These eleven contributions come from gifted pastors and teachers who are dedicated to connecting the serious study of scripture with the life of the church in the world. Each contributor shares the conviction that Amos deserves to be read and heard as a word of God for contemporary people of faith.

I am grateful to the contributors to this volume who have shared with us their insight into the texts of Amos. Their contributions represent a delightful and intentional diversity that is characteristic of the people of faith. Thanks also go to Mrs. Jackie Riley of the Editorial Division of Smyth & Helwys for her significant assistance in copyediting this book. This book would not have been completed without her careful attention to detail.

At the end of the twentieth century, the church will greatly benefit from a study of the eighth-century prophet Amos. Although the prophet's words were not easy to hear in his day and are certainly not easy to hear now, they are necessary words for "those who are at ease in Zion" in any generation. Amos reminds us that justice and righteousness are fundamental characteristics of the people of faith. Without them, the people of God are God's people in name only. Amos's challenge is that our worship of God become enfleshed in the "everdayness" of life as it relates to our neighbors.

But let justice roll down like waters,
and righteousness like an everflowing stream.
(Amos 5:24)

In this challenge Amos would have found great companionship with another prophet who challenged the people of Israel eight centuries later: Jesus of Nazareth. It was this Jesus who taught his followers that a vital relationship with God is completely wrapped up in how we relate to our neighbors.

> *Truly I tell you, just as you did it to one*
> *of the least of these who are members of my family, you did it to me.*
> (Matt 25:40)

I hope this publication will prove useful for pastors and teachers who turn to Amos with teaching and preaching in mind. May this collection stimulate listening, conversation, and encouragement to all who listen for a contemporary word from God from the book of Amos.

Cecil P. Staton, Jr.
Macon, Gerogia
Summer, 1995

Chapter One

Introducing
the Book of Amos

Mark E. Biddle

Introduction

The book of Amos appears as the third of the twelve minor prophets, after the prophets Isaiah, Jeremiah, Ezekiel, Daniel, Hosea, and Joel. This position belies the priority of the book in many respects. In fact, of the fifteen prophetic books in the Old Testament, Amos is almost certainly the oldest. Amos was the pioneer among the great eighth-century prophets of Israel and Judah: Hosea, Isaiah, and Micah.

Many readers throughout the ages have found his message and language harsh, his outlook critical and pessimistic. Yet, Amos was the first to prophesy the Assyrian conquest of the Northern Kingdom, the first to offer a sustained and consistent critique of Israelite society, the first to clearly and powerfully call God's people to an awareness of the need for national repentance, and the first to explain that election as God's people brings with it extraordinary responsibility. In short, Amos's message deserves very serious study, indeed. Without Amos's pioneering effort, our understanding of God's will for the chosen people, whether in the eighth century B.C. or the very late twentieth century A.D., would be much poorer.

The Man

We know the prophet Amos only through his book, which is more interested in the message than the messenger. The book tells us that he tended sycamore trees (7:14) and bred sheep (1:1; 7:14). The rare Hebrew term used in the second case (*noqed*), which is not the usual term for simple shepherd, suggests that he may have been something like a minor official in the royal Judean agriculture department. His home in Tekoa (now Khirbet Teku'a) lay ten miles south of Jerusalem, at the edge of the hilly Judean desert, poised just above the steep incline that descends eastward to the floor of the Jordan River Valley some 3,000 feet below.

We know nothing about Amos's personal life, and we can only speculate about his character. He was likely neither wealthy nor poor, accustomed to the simple life of hard work, and shaped by perspectives gained from life in close association with the land and one's neighbors. His life in the rugged country surrounding Tekoa may also have influenced his language.

Amos seems to have had no interest in sparing the feelings of his audience or in catering to their sense of culture and propriety. He spoke straightforwardly, pointedly, and often, harshly: "Hear this word, you cows of Bashan!" (Bashan was known for its rich pastureland and its sleek, well-fed cows. In effect, Amos called the women of Samaria "big, fat cows"—not exactly the most polite greeting.) Luxury, leisure, hypocrisy, and indifference—city life—would have seemed as unnatural to him as it does today to many people with roots in rural and suburban settings. For him, right was right and wrong was wrong, and taking advantage of the unfortunate fell clearly in the second category. He valued decency, honesty, faith, and compassion.

The Prophet

While the book of Amos devotes little attention to Amos's professional and personal life, it reveals a great deal about his vocation. At some point, Amos became aware of, and ultimately acted upon, a strong compulsion to speak out against the injustices and hypocrisies of life in Israel, Judah's northern neighbor. Several times Amos stressed that he did not choose this course of action (3:8), he had not prepared for it (7:14), and he was not trained as a spokesman for God (7:15). Instead, God gave him a message to preach. When the lion roars, people jump in fright; when God says preach, you jump to preach.

Amos's unwillingness to call himself a prophet, especially noteworthy in the exchange at Bethel with the priest Amaziah (7:10-17), may be attributed to the ambiguity of prophecy prior to the careers of Amos and the other great eighth-century figures (Hosea, Isaiah, and Micah). The Hebrew language has three terms to describe at least four different phenomena (*ro'eh, chozeh, nabi*).

Visionary?

Some prophets, such as Samuel, were visionaries or oracles (usually described with the Hebrew terms *ro'eh* or *chozeh*, both meaning "seer"). Often in return for compensation, they brought God's response to questions seeking God's advice or will on a matter (cf. Saul seeking Samuel's advice on finding his father's lost animals, 1 Sam 9–10). The Old Testament frequently mentions people going "to inquire of the Lord," always either through a priest who would employ the Urim and Thummim stones to render a yes/no answer, or through visionary prophets who could give answers to more complicated questions. To be sure, later "classical" prophets such as Amos had visionary experiences (cf. Isa 6; Ezek 1), but these experiences were not the norm for them, and their role far exceeded that of advisor in matters of lost property (cf. 1 Sam 9:9). In fact, the "classical" prophets seemed aware of the dangers involved in purchasing advice and opinions on God's will.

> Thus says the Lord concerning the prophets who lead my people astray, who cry "Peace" when they have something to eat, but declare war against those who put nothing into their mouths. Therefore it shall be night to you, without vision, and darkness to you, without revelation. The sun shall go down upon the prophets, and the day shall be black over them; the seers shall be disgraced, and the diviners put to shame; they shall all cover their lips, for there is no answer from God. (Mic 3:5-7)

The book of Amos reports a series of visions, too, although these visions seem very much to have the character of object lessons, not of mystical experience. Amos seems to have seen objects and events in his ordinary daily life as parables of God's message for Israel. Seeing locusts and then fire, Amos heard God's word of warning concerning the destruction of Israel. A carpenter squaring a wall with a plumbline became the occasion for God to remind Amos that Israel, too, would be measured to test whether it was straight and true. Seeing a basket of summer fruit (*kayitz*), he heard God's warning that the harvest, indeed the end (*ketz*), was near for Israel.

Ecstatic?

Other prophets in Israel's ancient past were known for their ecstatic spirituality (cf. 1 Sam 10:5-6, 10-13). Apparently, these "ecstatic" prophets lived and traveled in groups under the guidance of a teacher who was called their "father" (1 Sam 10:12; 2 Kgs 9:1). Their unusual behavior elicited from the people both a reverential awe and a degree of contempt (cf. 1 Sam 10:11-12; 2 Kgs 9:11).

Again, the classical prophets occasionally exhibited characteristically ecstatic behaviors. For example, Isaiah went about naked (Isa 20:2-4), and Ezekiel lay in a trance (Ezek 3:26-27; 33:21-22). Ecstatic spirituality was even less characteristic of the "classical" prophets than were visions, however; the book of Amos neither reports nor evidences that Amos had these experiences. Indeed, Amos denies membership in any prophetic school with his claim, "I am no prophet, nor a prophet's son" (7:14).

Royal Advisor?

A third group that could be described as prophets were professional religious advisors to the king. In the Ancient Near East, kings generally consulted prophets and priests before any major undertaking, and the prophets and priests typically told the kings what they wanted to hear. The classical prophets, especially Jeremiah, scorned these professionals as "prophets of peace" (Jer 6:13-14) and "lying prophets" (Jer 23:9-40, esp. v. 25), yes-men always willing to endorse the status quo no matter how corrupt or diseased it might be. 1 Kings 22 offers a particularly detailed look at the work of these professionals.

King Ahab sought the advice of his court prophets on the wisdom of going to war with Syria, although he had already made his decision and was not to be dissuaded, as history shows. Of course, the prophets wholeheartedly endorsed his decision—all but Micah ben Imlah. He foretold the king's death and the defeat of the combined armies of Israel and Judah, charging that the professionals were, in fact, false prophets. In turn, Ahab renounced Micah as a nay-saying thorn-in-the-flesh and obstinately marched to the battle in which he lost his life.

Independent Spokesperson for God

Although there had been a few precursors (Elijah, Micah ben Imlah, and others), Amos was the first of the so-called "classical" prophets. These thoroughly independent spokespersons (*nebi'im*, the term could also be applied to the other types of "prophets") for God belonged to no previously known categories. There is little wonder, then, that Amos so vigorously rejected the title "prophet" or that Amaziah, the priest of the royal sanctuary in Bethel, had difficulty classifying and dealing with him (Amos 7). Here was an apparently normal man—in no one's employ, unable to be bought, associated with no prophetic school, not prone to sensational religious experiences, uninterested in pleasing the king with the official interpretation of current events—determined only to speak the abrupt truth about Israel's sinful condition and the coming punishment.

His Career and Times

We do not know the age of Amos, whether he was married, or whether he had children. Yet, the book provides solid clues that, together with what we know of the period from extrabiblical sources, allow us to describe the historical context of his ministry with some certainty.

Date

The superscription to the book of Amos mentions two kings whose reigns can be dated with relative certainty. Jeroboam II of Israel enjoyed a long reign from the mid-780s to the mid-740s B.C. Uzziah of Judah also reigned for several decades. He died in the late 740s after suffering from leprosy the last years of his life. As a result, he had installed his son Jotham as co-regent from about 750 B.C. Since the superscription to the book does not mention Jotham, we can assume that it refers to the period before the onset of Uzziah's leprosy. At the other extreme, the superscription also mentions an earthquake (see also Zech 14:5), likely the earthquake detected in the archeological evidence from excavations at Hazor and other sites. The Hazor evidence suggests a date of around 760 for this disaster. The possible reference (Amos 8:9) to the solar eclipse of June 763 B.C. may also provide additional confirmation that Amos was active after 760. Amos's career can probably be placed, then, in the period between 760 and 750 B.C.

Career

We know very little about the duration or circumstances of Amos's career. From the evidence provided by the book itself, we can only deduce that at some time in the 750s, Amos, compelled solely by the conviction that he must deliver God's message to Israel, left his Judean country home to preach in the North. Judging from the contents of the book, he must have made a circuit of two, perhaps three, leading cities: Bethel, the site of one of two royal temples in the North (3:14; 4:4; 5:5-6; 7:10); Samaria, the seat of Israel's government (3:9; 4:1; 6:1); and perhaps Gilgal (4:4; 5:5). Also judging from the contents of the book, he probably delivered several short pronouncements and declarations, since many of the units preserved in the book are relatively short and self-contained.

We can speculate that his ministry may have been measured in months and probably lasted no longer than one to two years. We know that he came to the attention of royal officials (Amos 7) who regarded him as an agitator; but we know neither the outcome of this encounter nor the manner in which Amos concluded his ministry. Presumably, after (forcefully) delivering the message God had sent him to deliver, he returned to Tekoa.

The International Situation

What could Amos have noted in the circumstances of Israel's national life that so disturbed him? On the international stage, Israel was enjoying a period of calm almost unrivaled since it had seceded from the Davidic monarchy in about 926 B.C. (cf. 1 Kgs 12). Throughout much of the century before Amos appeared, Israel had been engaged in a series of border wars. Immediately following the division of the United Kingdom, there had been a number of border skirmishes between Israel and Judah (1 Kgs 15:16). The kings of both nations apparently sought to reunite the kingdom by conquest, but their forces were too evenly matched, and they soon came to accept the division as a given.

Israel's most threatening enemy was Syria to the northeast. The kings of Damascus were often interested in expanding their kingdom. Syro-Israelite conflicts centered especially around Syria's competing claims to Gilead, Israel's Transjordanian territory (2 Kgs 12ff). The Ammonites, situated on the other side of Gilead (to the South) from the Syrians (to the North), seem to have regarded Israel's struggles with Syria as an opportunity to carve off some of Gilead for themselves. Amos refers to Israel's difficulties with both of these neighbors in his preaching (1:3-5, 13-15).

When Jeroboam II assumed the throne, however, the Syrian threat was diminishing. The Assyrians farther to Syria's east had just entered a period of decline. The great Assyrian emperor Tiglath-Pileser III would not assume the throne and begin his career of foreign conquest until 745 B.C. While many of the small nations in the region—including Israel—were able to enjoy this period of Assyrian decline, the Syrians were now occupied with their aggressive northern neighbor, Hamath. Israel, at peace with Judah and untroubled by the Syrians, had already begun to rebuild even before Jeroboam assumed the throne. His predecessor, Jehoash, began reclaiming conquered Israelite territory (2 Kgs 13:25), and Jeroboam was soon able to complete the liberation (2 Kgs 14:25). It remained for him to rule over Israel in a time of remarkable peace.

The Domestic Situation

Israel's domestic situation also seemed unusually promising and prosperous. All the evidence points to a time of economic growth. Amos himself described the scene. Commerce was booming (2:6-8; 8:5-6). A market for fine imported textiles, furnitures, and carvings had developed (3:12; 6:4-6). Sectors of society had acquired substantial wealth. Some were living lives of leisure and luxury (6:4-6). There was a building boom (3:10-11, 15; 5:11). Public markets and royal sanctuaries were busy, always a sign of economic vitality (4:4-5; 5:21-23; 8:5-6). Yet this very prosperity, like the feverish activity of the acutely ill, was itself symptomatic of Israel's disease.

His Message

Amos's message seems to focus on three major accusations: (1) the oppression of the poor through the corruption of justice, (2) the carefree enjoyment of extravagant luxury by some, and (3) the disjointed relationship between a vigorous religious life and the claims of social justice. In order to best understand these accusations, we must remember the structure of Israel's social and economic life as prescribed in the covenant.

Background

Israel began as a purely agrarian culture and continued so for centuries. These former shepherds and Egyptian slaves lived in the sparsely populated, semi-arid hills of Palestine in an age before industrialization, consumer-driven commerce, and service professions. With the exception of royal officials, priests, and a few craftsmen who lived in the cities, Israelites could not hope to sustain themselves and provide for their families except by farming and rearing small livestock. The key to economic viability, then, was the land. Furthermore, Israel's experience in Egypt had taught it the hard lessons of oppression and slavery. The Israelites were determined never again to live as slaves or to allow their fellow Israelites to do so.

The Mosaic covenant includes a number of provisions designed to address related issues. These provisions were based on the theological premises that God had delivered Israel from slavery to be a free people (Lev 26:13; Deut 7:8; 15:15; 17:16; cf. 1 Sam 8:17-18) and that the land God had promised them belonged to God—they had been granted use of it as an inheritance, but it was still, in fact, God's (Lev 25:23-24; cf. Deut 19:14; Josh 14:1-5).

Practically, these two theological claims gave birth to a series of laws and institutions, all designed to maintain an awareness that the land was God's and that Israel should be free. The most basic principle of the covenant in this regard involved the notion that land could not be bought or sold (Lev 25:23-24). Strictly speaking, after all, individual Israelites did not own the land they inherited: it was God's. Furthermore, without land, they could not sustain themselves.

These dual interests in affirming God's ultimate ownership and in protecting universal access to the means of production also underlie the laws governing the Sabbath and Jubilee years. At most, land could be effectively rented for periods of up to six years, or until the next Sabbath or Jubilee year. It was then to be returned to its original owner (Lev 25:25-34). Debts were forgiven in Sabbath and Jubilee years (Exod 21:1-11; Deut 15:1-18), and Israelites who had been sold by their creditors as debt slaves were also released in the next Sabbath or Jubilee year (Lev 25:10-17, 39-55). Provisions for the return of other types of personal belongings such as clothing offered to creditors as collateral were even stricter. They must be returned to the original owner by sundown of the same day to prevent the wealthy from taking advantage of the less fortunate (Exod 22:26-27; Deut 24:10-13; cf. Amos 2:8). The personal dignity of every member of God's chosen people was highly valued.

God's covenant with Israel went to even greater lengths to insure that all Israelites would be able to provide for their families. While land and debt slaves must be returned and set free in the next Sabbath year, the nearest male relative (the *go'el*, or kinsman-redeemer/avenger) of the dislocated individual was under covenantal obligation to secure the return of the land or the release of the relative—particularly to pay the debt—as soon as he became aware of the situation (Lev 25). The *go'el* was not to permit his relative to be disenfranchised for one moment longer than necessary.

The institution of levirate marriage fulfilled a similar function. In the ancient world, in a society that did not normally permit women to inherit their husband's property and before the advent of social security, the death of a childless man presented a particularly difficult problem. First, his property would be ownerless, and second, his widow would be without means of support. The covenant provided for the solution to both of these problems through the levirate marriage. The deceased's nearest male relative was *required* to marry the widow and to father a child who would be considered the legal heir of the deceased. The child would take possession of his deceased "father's" property and would be able thus to provide for his mother (Deut 25:5-10; cf. Gen 38; Ruth).

The Mosaic covenant goes to extravagant lengths, then, to ensure that no Israelite should become permanently destitute, disenfranchised, or dislocated. Yet, Amos explicitly addresses several cases of social injustices in direct contradiction to the system prescribed in the covenant (2:6-8; 5:10-13; 8:5-6). How could this be?

Social Indictment

The book of Amos assumes an understanding of developments in Israelite society of which we have no direct evidence. We can only suggest two possibilities. Segments of Israelite society may have found ways to subvert the legal system. Several passages in the book of Amos and in the book of his younger near-contemporary Micah at least hint at such subversions of covenant law (Amos 3:10; 5:10, 12, 15, 24; 8:6; Mic 2:2; 3:1-3, 11). On the other hand, the pressures of increased population and urbanization may have resulted in property holdings too small to support families. In this case, wealthier Israelites would have willingly offered credit, knowing all along that their poorer neighbors would be unable to repay. When debts mounted, the creditors would have taken advantage of the opportunity to convert the small holdings of land and, apparently, even the small landholders themselves into cash (Amos 2:6-8; 8:6).

Amos addressed his message primarily to those wealthy absentee landlords who made their fortunes through the exploitation and ruin of day laborers and poor farmers. Amos's audience lived by reducing independent Israelite farmers into "sharecroppers" and indentured servants.

Amos measured Israelite society by the standards of the covenant and of common decency and found the people wanting on both counts. Even when the leisure class observed the letter of the law, it violated its spirit and the ideas of fairness and decency common to all human beings. While it may have been technically legal to sell a person into six years of slavery because he owed for a pair of sandals, only the most callous opportunist would have done so. Neither the sense of community and neighborliness Amos must have known in Tekoa, nor the ideal of freedom under God revealed in the covenant, governed Israel's marketplace. Only the fit, or better the fortunate, would survive.

What would Amos say about our society's "buyer beware," "charge what the market will bear," and "pay only the wage that you must" economy? What would he say about for-profit hospitals, leveraged buy-outs, and homeless children? What would he say about record corporate profits and stagnant workers' wages?

Religious Indictment

Amos said very little about Israel's religious life, in the limited sense, but his few remarks were scathing (2:8; 4:4-5; 5:4-5, 21-27). In Amos's view, the forms of worship, even when enthusiastically and regularly practiced, lack sincerity and validity if the lives of the worshipers show no evidence of understanding that the God they worship is righteous and holy. In fact, Israel's unique relationship with God only increased the nation's responsibility to do justice (3:1-2). To sing doxologies praising God's holiness without living holy lives, to offer sacrifice for forgivness of sin without repenting of it, is to insult and mock God (5:21-27).

In this regard, it is interesting to note that Amos's later contemporary, Hosea, a native Israelite prophet, concentrated almost exclusively on Israel's religious life in his preaching. Israel's problem, in his view, was not primarily its unjust social order, but its adulterous relationship with God. The Israelites did not truly know him; they were not devoted to him; they did not love him. In a way it seems odd that two prophets could preach to the same people in the same period and see such differences. For the one, Israel's society was unjust; for the other, Israel's faith in God was unsound. Years later, the prophet Jeremiah echoed the messages of both prophets in a single statement:

> Will you steal, murder, commit adultery, swear falsely, make offerings to Baal, and go after other gods that you have not known, and then come and stand before me in this house, which is called by my name, and say, "We are safe!"? (Jer 7:9-10)

Later still, Israel's greatest prophet clearly described the relationship between these two elements of the life of faith when he summarized the whole law:

> You shall love the Lord your God with all your heart, and with all your soul, and with all your mind, and with all your strength. . . . You shall love your neighbor as yourself. (Mark 12:30-31)

Could we hypothesize that when people lead unjust public and social lives (Israel in Amos's view), they do not truly know or love God (Israel in Hosea's view)? Can we judge our hearts by our deeds (Matt 7:15-20)?

Verdict

At any rate, Amos's diagnosis of Israel's disease allowed for only one prognosis: punishment. The day of the Lord, when God takes to the battlefield against God's enemies, is soon approaching. For centuries, Israel had welcomed this day as a time of deliverance from its enemies (Isa 13:6, 9, 13; Jer 46:10; 47:4; Ezek 30:3; Obad 15; against Israel Isa 2:9ff; Zeph 1:7ff, 14ff; 2:2-3; 3:8). Amos warned that this time, however, God's enemy will be Israel. Israel will be defeated in battle. God will fight against God's own people (5:18-21). The plumbline has revealed a crooked wall that must be torn down (7:7-9). History has proven Amos true. Under Sargon II, the Assyrians conquered Israel, destroyed Samaria, and led many away captive in 722 B.C., a short thirty years after Amos's ministry.

His Book

The book of Amos exhibits a rather sophisticated structure governed by the grouping of materials according to common literary features and, to a degree, by the development of an argument. Originally, the materials in the book were probably delivered as short sayings over a period of time and probably not in the order in which they now appear. As the third-person superscription to the book (1:1) and the brief biographical narrative (7:10-17) suggest, Amos's preaching was probably collected and edited by someone other than the prophet himself—perhaps pious scribes or priests convinced that his message should be preserved for posterity.

Some scholars see evidence that a few sayings concerning the southern kingdom of Judah may have also been included as supplements when the book was prepared for publication. Roughly the second half of the book, beginning with the biographical section, seems to be less consistently arranged than the first half. Some scholars see this breakdown in structure as evidence that the book underwent several revisions before attaining its present form. At any rate, when analyzed carefully, the book represents a balanced literary composition that should be interpreted as a whole.

The book of Amos can be outlined in several ways. The outline below is a hybrid attempt to reflect both the groups of literary genre and the development of the argument. It calls particular attention to four formulas that dominate, beginning in 3:1. In chapters 3–5, the formula "Hear this word!" appears at the head of three major subsections; it is joined by a fourth appearance toward the end of the book (8:4). Two "woe" oracles occur next in sequence (5:18-27; 6:1-4). The biographical narrative (7:10-17) interrupts a series of four visions (7:1–8:3). After the narrative, the fourth vision is followed by reprise occurrences of the "Hear this word!" formula and a fifth and final vision. They alternate with placement of two new elements: the "behold the days are coming" and "in that day" sayings. These new elements occur twice each in an ABB'A' pattern, so that the end of the book (especially after the narrative) assumes an intricate shape: vision, hear, behold, in that day, vision, in that day, behold (ABCD A'D'C').

The argument of the book develops with equal intricacy. After the superscription, the intriguing foreword already sets the tone for the book: The Lord roars and vegetation wilts; God is obviously angry, but at whom? Immediately the extended series of sayings against the nations of the region seem to provide the answer. Amos addresses first Israel's neighbors to the northeast, then to the southwest, then to the northwest, and so on until finally all of Israel's neighbors, even Judah, have heard of God's displeasure. And then, in a way that must have startled Amos's original audience, he turns his attention to Israel, which is grouped with the pagan nations as equally—but no more—deserving of God's anger.

So, God rules over all of human history. God sees injustice and wrong wherever it occurs, but Amos makes also a more subtle claim. On what basis does God judge the Syrians and the Edomites? They do not know God's revealed will; they were not parties to Israel's covenant with God. Does God still hold them accountable for observing its provisions? Of course not, but God does apparently hold all human beings accountable for standards of decent and humane behavior that are the common heritage of the human race. Amos does not develop a doctrine of the conscience or of general revelation of God's moral will in the human psyche, but he does seem to assume that even Ammonites should know that it is despicable to slash open pregnant women, even in wartime!

If God holds the pagans to this simple, common standard, what must God expect of the chosen people who have the Torah of Moses? Amos turns immediately to this issue in 3:1. Because God has special concern for the Israelites, God expects their behavior to meet a standard far exceeding mere common decency. Parents expect the best behavior of their own children. Amos levels a stinging accusation against Israel: Even the pagans understand justice well enough to assess your behavior. They know right from wrong better than you (3:9-15)!

What is Israel's sin? Greed, unjust treatment of the poor, wanton luxury (4:1-3). Punishment is inevitable (4:4-13). Amos begins Israel's funeral (5:1-3) since Israel's religion, empty as it is of the fruits of right-eousness, will not protect the nation from God's justice (5:4-17). The pair of "woe" sayings (5:18–6:14) reiterates these themes: Israel will be punished in the Day of the Lord; its worship is hollow; the bounty and extravagance that some enjoy will be stripped away.

The cycle of four visions that surround the report of the encounter between Amos and Amaziah deals with Amos's growing conviction that Israel's downfall has become inevitable. Amos persuades God to relent of the locust plague and the firestorm, but when God measures Israel with the plumbline and finds the people crooked and distorted, Amos realizes that the verdict has been reached and the sentence will soon be executed. Indeed, the harvest is near.

For the most part, the cycle that follows the fourth vision repeats the charges and verdict already reached. The wealthy in Israel love profit more than they love God and fellow human beings. God's punishment is sure. In fact, God has already issued the order to tear Israel down. In an allusion to earlier portions of the book (1:3–2:16; 3:1), the final vision reminds Israel that its special relationship with God does not exempt it from God's demands for justice (9:7-10). The only new note occurs in the closing five verses of the book. Finally words of hope (9:11-15), although they hold little comfort for those who heard Amos preach, promise that beyond punishment God will still care for God's people. God will restore them and sustain them once again.

Outline of Amos

For Further Study

Anderson, Bernhard W. *The Eighth Century Prophets: Amos, Hosea, Isaiah, Micah.* Philadelphia: Fortress, 1978.

Andersen, F. I., and D. N. Freedman. *Amos: A New Translation with Introduction and Commentary.* Anchor Bible, vol. 24a. New York: Doubleday, 1989.

Andersen, Francis I. "Amos, Book of." *The Oxford Companion to the Bible.* Edited by Bruce M. Metzger and Michael D. Coogan. New York/Oxford: Oxford University Press, 1993.

Barré, Michael L. "Amos." *The New Jerome Biblical Commentary.* Edited by Raymond E. Brown, Joseph A. Fitzmyer, and Roland E. Murphy. Englewood Cliffs NJ: Prentice Hall, 1990.

Barstad, Hans M. *The Religious Polemics of Amos: Studies in the Preaching of Am 2,7B-8; 4,1-13; 5,1-27; 6,4-7; 8,14.* Vol. 4. *Supplements to Vetus Testamentum.* Leiden: E. J. Brill, 1984.

Carroll, Robert P. "Amos." *A Dictionary of Biblical Interpretation.* Edited by R. J. Coggins and J. L. Houlder. London: SCM Press; Philadelphia: Trinity Press International, 1990.

Cathcart, K. J. "Day of Yahweh." *The Anchor Bible Dictionary.* Edited by David Noel Freedman. New York: Doubleday, 1992.

Cerny, Ladislav. *The Day of Yahweh and Some Relevant Problems.* Prague: Nákladem Filosofické Fakulty University Karlovy, 1948.

Childs, Brevard S. "Amos." *Introduction to the Old Testament as Scripture.* Philadelphia: Fortress Press, 1979.

Cripps, Richard S. *A Critical and Exegetical Commentary on the Book of Amos.* London: SPCK, 1969.

Doorly, William J. *Prophet of Justice: Understanding the Book of Amos.* New York: Paulist, 1989.

Fosbroke, Hughell E. W., and Sidney Lovett. "The Book of Amos." *The Interpreter's Bible*, vol. 6. Edited by George Arthur Buttrick et al. New York and Nashville: Abingdon, 1956.

Greeven, Heinrich. "zēteō, zētēsis", ek-, epizēteō." *Theological Dictionary of the New Testament*, vol. 2. Edited by Gerhard Kittel. Translated and edited by Geoffrey W. Bromiley. Grand Rapids MI: Eerdmans, 1964 (orig. 1935).

Hammershaimb, Erling. *The Book of Amos: A Commentary*. Translated by John Sturdy. Oxford: Basil Blackwell, 1970.

Harper, William Rainey. *A Critical and Exegetical Commentary on Amos and Hosea*. International Critical Commentary. Edinburgh: T. & T. Clark, 1905.

Hasel, Gerhard F. *Understanding the Book of Amos: Basic Issues in Current Interpretations*. Grand Rapids MI: Baker, 1991.

Hiers, Richard H. 1992. "Day of the Lord." *The Anchor Bible Dictionary*. Edited by David Noel Freedman. New York: Doubleday, 1992.

Hoffmann, Yair. "The Day of the Lord as a Concept and a Term in the Prophetic Literature." *Zeitschrift für die alttestamentliche Wissenschaft*. 93:37-50.

Honeycutt, Roy Lee. *Amos and His Message: An Expository Commentary*. Nashville: Broadman, 1963.

Keil, C. F. *Minor Prophets*. Commentary on the Old Testament. Translated by James Martin. Grand Rapids MI: Eerdmans, 1978.

King, Philip J. "Amos." *The Jerome Biblical Commentary*, vol. 1. Edited by Raymond E. Brown, Joseph A. Fitzmyer, and Roland E. Murphy. Englewood Cliffs NJ: Prentice-Hall, 1968.

King, Philip J. *Amos, Hosea, Micah: An Archaeological Commentary*. Philadelphia: Westminster, 1988.

Kraft, Charles F. "The Book of Amos." *The Interpreter's One-Volume Commentary on the Bible.* Edited by Charles M. Laymon. Nashville/New York: Abingdon, 1971.

Marks, Herbert J. "The Twelve Prophets." *The Literary Guide to the Bible.* Edited by Robert Alter and Frank Kermode. Cambridge MA: Harvard University Press, 1987.

Marsh, John. *Amos and Micah: Thus Saith the Lord.* London: SCM, 1959.

Mays, James Luther. *Amos: A Commentary.* Old Testament Library. Philadelphia: Westminster, 1969.

Melugin, Roy F. "Amos." *Harper's Bible Commentary.* Edited by James L. Mays et al. San Francisco: Harper & Row, 1988.

Motyer, J. A. *The Message of Amos: The Day of the Lion.* Downers Grove IL: Intervarsity, 1974.

Myers, Jacob M. "The Book of Amos." *The Layman's Bible Commentary*, vol. 14. Edited by Balmer H. Kelly et al. Richmond VA: John Knox, 1959.

O'Brien, J. Randall. "Amos" and "Amos, Book of." *Mercer Dictionary of the Bible.* Edited by Watson E. Mills. Macon GA: Mercer University Press, 1990.

Paul, Shalom M. *Amos: A Commentary on the Book of Amos.* Hermeneia. Minneapolis: Fortress, 1991.

Rad, Gerhard von. "The Origin of the Concept of the Day of Yahweh." *Journal of Semitic Studies* 4 (1959): 97-108.

Robertson, James, and Carl E. Amerding. "Amos." *The International Standard Bible Encyclopedia*, vol. A–D. Edited by Geoffrey W. Bromiley et al. Grand Rapids MI: Eerdmans, 1979.

Robinson, Theodire H. *The Book of Amos. Hebrew Text Edited with Critical and Grammatical Notes.* Texts for Students 30. London: SPCK, 1923, 1951.

Rosenbaum, Stanley N. *Amos of Israel. A New Interpretation.* Macon GA: Mercer University Press, 1990.

Sanderson, Judith E. "Amos." *The Women's Bible Commentary.* Edited by Carol A. Newsom and Sharon H. Ringe. London: SPCK; Louisville: Westminster/John Knox Press, 1992.

Shelley, John C. "Amos." *Mercer Commentary on the Bible.* Edited by Watson E. Mills et al. Macon GA: Mercer University Press, 1994.

Sizemore, Burlan A., Jr. "Judgment upon Israel (Amos, Hosea)." *The Centuries of Decline.* Bible Survey Series 5. Nashville: Convention Press, 1970.

Smith, Billy K. "Hosea, Joel, Amos, Obadiah, Jonah." *Layman's Bible Book Commentary*, vol. 13. Nashville: Broadman, 1982.

Smith, George Adam. *The Book of the Twelve Prophets Commonly Called the Minor*, vol. 1. *Amos, Hosea, and Micah, with an Introduction and a Sketch of Prophecy in Early Israel.* The Expositors' Bible. New York: Hodder & Stoughton and George H. Doran Co., 1896; 2nd ed., New York: Harper, 1928.

Smith, Ralph L. "Amos." *The Broadman Bible Commentary*, vol. 7. Edited by Clifton J. Allen et al. Nashville: Broadman, 1972.

Snaith, Norman H. *Amos, Hosea, and Micah.* Epworth Preacher's Commentaries. London: Epworth Press, 1956.

————. *The Book of Amos.* Part 1. *Introduction.* Study Notes on Bible Books. London: Epworth, 1945, 1957.

————. *The Book of Amos.* Part 2. *Translation and Notes.* Study Notes on Bible Books. London: Epworth, 1946, 1958.

Stuart, Douglas. *Hosea-Jonah.* Word Biblical Themes. Dallas: Word, 1989.

Wagner, Siegfried. "*darash, midhrash.*" *Theological Dictionary of the Old Testament*, vol. 3. Edited by G. Johannes Botterweck and Helmer Ringgren. Translated by John T. Willis, Geoffrey W. Bromiley, and David E. Green. Grand Rapids MI: Eerdmans, 1978.

Watts, John D. W. *Vision and Prophecy in Amos.* Grand Rapids MI: Eerdmans, 1958.

Weiss, Meir. "The Origin of the 'Day of the Lord'—reconsidered." *Hebrew Union College Annual* 37 (1966): 29-72.

Wolff, Hans Walter. *Amos the Prophet: The Man and His Background.* Translated by Foster R. McCurley. Philadelphia: Fortress, 1973.

————. *Joel and Amos: A Commentary on the Books of the Prophets Joel and Amos.* Translated by Waldemar Janzen, S. Dean McBride, Jr., and Charles A. Muenchow. Hermeneia. Philadelphia: Fortress, 1977.

Chapter Two

"Thus Says the Lord
'Is It Not Indeed So?' "
Amos 1–2

Cecil P. Staton, Jr.

Background

Structure

The book of Amos, like most Old Testament prophetic books, begins with a superscription (see, for example, the first verses of Isaiah, Jeremiah, Hosea, and Micah). Following the superscription, Amos's readers listen in on a lengthy sermon of sorts (1:2–2:16), one of Amos's best. In this brief prophetic sermon, readers are taken on a rollercoaster journey back and forth to Israel's neighbors, including a stop at Judah. Only after Israel is completely encircled does the prophetic sermon stop at Israel and reveal its dramatic climax. Israel too must face impending judgment. Israel is no different than its neighbors, no different than Judah, and receives the very same indictment. Judgment is a foregone conclusion. This indictment of Israel's neighbors, Judah, and finally Israel itself must stand among the best and most dramatic prophetic writings in the Old Testament and is the subject of this chapter.

Superscription (1:1)

Most Old Testament prophetic writings begin with a superscription (see exceptions Obadiah and Jonah). Although some are brief (see Joel,

Nahum, and Habakkuk), prophetic superscriptions usually include information that sets the prophet into a historical context, and occasionally some additional but limited biographical or contextual information. Very likely, supersciptions were not part of the original books themselves, but were added at a later time to provide helpful information about historical context for later generations of readers and hearers.

The superscription to the book of Amos includes information concerning Amos's original occupation and a historical context for the material. Amos is described as being "among the shepherds of Tekoa." The Hebrew words translated "shepherd" may mean more than the simple image conjured up by the English word, or by remembrances of David, or even the shepherds of Christmas. Amos may have been somewhat more prominent than this, though it is difficult to be sure. In 7:14 he is described as "a herdsman and a dresser of sycamore trees." Some scholars speculate that Amos held an administrative, perhaps governmental, position with considerable authority. The contents of the book taken as a whole suggest a literate individual with knowledge of both the excesses of the upper class and the tremendous need among the abused poor. In any case, clearly Amos was not a professional prophet, but was "snatched" or "seized" to become a prophet of harsh words in a smooth age.

The superscription references two kings: Uzziah of Judah and Jeroboam II of Israel. Uzziah reigned over Israel from approximately 783–742 B.C., although his son reigned as co-regent from about 750 after the king contracted leprosy. Jeroboam II reigned over Israel from 786–746 B.C. "Two years before the earthquake" may be a reference to a natural upheaval that may be detected by archaeological evidence and dated approximately 760 B.C., though this is not certain. Most scholars date the period of Amos's ministry to approximately 760–750 B.C.

During this period, Syria was the immediate power to the north and east, while still further north and east there was Assyria. During this decade, Assyria was not a menace to Palestine. It was too weak domestically to cause trouble abroad. This was also a time of peaceful coexistence for Israel and Judah. In the midst of this void of outside political influence, both Israel and Judah prospered. Amos describes an economic polarization between the wealthy class and the poor. This was also a religious time, according to Amos. Many people flocked to the cultic centers of Bethel and Gilgal to offer their sacrifices. Apparently many of them viewed prosperity as a sign of God's blessing.

Yet little thought was given to the moral and ethical responsibilities that the blessed and prosperous should feel toward their neighbors. Much of Amos's preaching, as in this first great sermon, is a challenge to Israel to remember that relationship with and blessing from God were not merely a privilege to be enjoyed by the wealthy few, but brought considerable responsibility to those with much for those less fortunate. From the beginning, Amos makes no bones about the purpose of his ministry. "The LORD roars from Zion, and utters his voice from Jerusalem" (1:2). This likely editorial description (see Joel 3:16; Jer 25:30) stands as the theme for what follows. Yahweh's response to Israel is nothing less than a "roar." There is little positive here. Amos is a prophet of Yahweh's judgment.

Sermon Content

Amos's sermon makes seven stops before coming home to Israel. Each stop or point in this prophetic sermon announces an indictment of one of Israel's neighbors and then describes the punishment that will most assuredly come.

1:3-5 concerns Israel's immediate neighbor to the northeast, Damascus, the capital of Syria. Hazael and Ben-hadad III were rulers of Syria[1] (see 2 Kgs 13:3). Because of atrocities committed in the Syrian conquest of Gilead (2 Kgs 10:32-33), a mountainous region located between the Dead Sea and the Sea of Galilee, Syria is indicted. Its horrendous treatment of its neighbor will result in the destruction of Damascus and the exile of its inhabitants.

1:6-8 turns to Gaza, Ashdod, Ashkelon, and Ekron—four Philistine cities along the southwest coast of Palestine. These Philistine strongholds are indicted for their slave traffic with Edom (southwest corner of Palestine; see 2 Chron 21:16-17; Joel 3:4-8; Zeph 2:4-7). For their atrocities these cities shall themselves know destruction and exile.

1:9-10 takes the reader to the northern coast of Palestine, the region of Tyre. Tyre is indicted because it too broke the "covenant of kinship" by handing over entire communities to Edom (see Joel 3:4-8). Thus Tyre's wall shall burn, and its strongholds be devoured.

1:11-12 concerns Edom in the southeast corner of Palestine. Edom is indicted because "he pursued his brother with the sword and cast off all pity; he maintained his anger perpetually, and kept his wrath forever." Edom too will know fire and devastation.

1:13-15 turns to the Ammonites. Ammon lay east of the Jordan and northeast of the Dead Sea. Ammon is indicted because of inhuman atrocities against the women of Gilead in an attempt to enlarge its territory. Ammon will know fire, destruction, and exile as a result of its actions, nothing less than the storm on the day of the whirlwind and the shouting of the day of battle.

2:1-3 turns to Moab, east of the Dead Sea between Edom and Ammon. Moab is indicted for desecrating the tomb of the king of Edom. As a result, Moab "shall die amid uproar, amid shouting and the sound of trumpet." Even all of the officials of the court will die with their king.

2:4-5 brings the reader to Judah, Israel's brother and immediate neighbor to the south. Judah is indicted because it has rejected Yahweh's law—Yahweh's statutes have not been kept. The current citizens of Judah have continued in the same destructive paths of their ancestors, so Yahweh will send fire on Judah and destroy its strongholds.

The drama of Amos 1:3–2:16 is now clear. Israel has been encircled. The prophet has voiced Yahweh's indictment and sounded Yahweh's punishment for all of Israel's neighbors. From Damascus (northeast) to Gaza (southwest), Tyre (northwest) to Edom (southeast), Ammon (west) to Moab (southwest), and finally to Judah (south), all of the significant players in the life and world of Israel have been singled out for indictment and judgment.

Imagine the scene. The upstart prophet from Judah has come north to preach. Perhaps the setting is the town square or city gate. Passersby have stopped to hear this entertaining street preacher called Amos. At least he was entertaining. He was certainly letting Israel's neighbors have it. This was the kind of preaching any patriotic Israelite could say "amen" to. But Amos's sermon was not over. There was one final point to make in this most dramatic of prophetic sermons.

2:6-16. Laughter and hearty amens now give way to shocked silence as Amos moves in for the climatic point of his sermon. "Thus says the LORD: For three transgressions of Israel, and for four, I will not revoke the punishment . . . " What is Yahweh's indictment of Israel?

Israel's difficult lesson is that the nation will be judged by the very same standards as its neighbors. When weighed in the balances, Israel's sins are just as significant as its neighbors'. Yahweh hands down an indictment against Israel "because they sell the righteous for silver, and the needy for a pair of sandals—they who trample the head of the poor into the dust of the earth, and push the afflicted out of the way."

If it is possible, however, Israel is even more guilty. Like Judah, Israel is the possessor of a special relationship with Yahweh. "I brought you up out of the land of Egypt, and led you forty years in the wilderness . . . I raised up some of your children to be prophets and some of your youths to be nazirites." Israel has no excuse. "Is it not indeed so, O people of Israel? says the LORD."

Yet Israel has caused the nazirites to break their vows and has forbidden the prophets to prophesy (2:12). So there is now no hope. Amos's sermon ends with swift judgment. Israel will be run over. "So, I will press you down in your place, just as a cart presses down when it is full of sheaves." The fast will loose their swiftness, the strong their strength, the horsemen their lives, and the stout of heart their strength. Amos's sermon ends on a tragic note. The people of God who have no excuse will experience Yahweh's swift judgment.

What can they say? What answer can they offer to the charge? Israel, the people of God no less, have forgotten that relationship with God is only as good as relationship with neighbor. They stand charged. Amos's audience is quiet. You could hear a pin drop. "Is it not indeed so, O People of Israel? says the LORD."

Application for Preaching and Teaching

"Thus Says the Lord: 'Is It Not Indeed So?' "
Amos 1:3–2:11; 1 John 3:11

Introduction

Amos of Tekoa stands at the beginning of a list of enormously important prophetic figures who came upon the scene of ancient Israelite
history about the middle of the eighth century before Christ. Amos
was in many ways a pioneer. He was followed closely in time and message by Hosea, Isaiah, and Micah.

The arrival of these interesting characters marks a significant transition in ancient Israelite prophecy. Their work marks the birth of the
period of classical prophecy, as it is sometimes called. This is the time
of the great writing prophets of Israel. This transition is of enormous
significance for several reasons. In the eighth-century prophets Amos,
Hosea, Isaiah, and Micah, we find older prophetic models being abandoned. Their ministries do not reflect previous Old Testament models
for prophecy. Before Amos there were visionary prophets who might
reveal God's answers to a question for a price. There were ecstatic
prophets with their traveling schools and known for their unusual
behavior. There were court prophets who served as royal advisors or
chaplains, but more often as the king's spiritual yes-men, adding divine
sanction to official political will.

In these prophets—again beginning with Amos—a transition
occurs. Amos is the first of the so-called "classical" prophets. While
some of the earlier types and characteristics of prophecy continue for
a while, we now encounter those prophetic figures who were
thoroughly independent spokespersons for God. In Amos we find
someone who is apparently a normal man—"in no one's employ,
unable to be bought, associated with no prophetic school, not prone to
sensational religious experiences, uninterested in pleasing the king
and the political establishment."[2] Here is a man boldly determined
only to speak the abrupt truth about Israel's sinful condition and the
fact that God cares about the behavior of God's people. God will not
sit idly by while God's people live as though their relationship with

God has little or no impact on how they live out their lives in the every-dayness of life.

Amos came on the scene sometime during the 950s B.C. We know very little about him except that he refers to himself as a tender of sycamore trees and a sheep breeder (1:1; 7:14)—or as my Old Testament professor B. Elmo Scoggin used to tell his classes, the Hebrew literally says he was a "fig-pinching sheep-poker." All the text reveals is that Amos, from the rugged Judean country town of Tekoa ten miles south of Jerusalem (in the Southern Kingdom), experienced a dramatic call to prophetic ministry.

As Amos recounts his "call" to action to Amaziah, the priest at Bethel, we capture something of the uniqueness of this prophet and the movement he begins: "I am no prophet, nor a prophet's son; but I am a herdsman, and a dresser of sycamore trees, and the LORD took me from following the flock, and the LORD said to me, 'Go, prophesy to my people Israel.'" (7:14-15).

So we get the picture. A "fig-pinching, sheep-poker," upstart preacher from a rural southern village crosses the border into the Northern Kingdom of Israel declaring he has received a message from Yahweh. Yet he has no official standing. By his own admission he has no pedigree. He is not a professional prophet nor part of a prophetic school. He certainly has no standing in the royal court. With all these obstacles to deter him, Amos leaves the comfort of his life in Tekoa and accepts the difficult assignment to be Yahweh's spokesperson preaching *harsh words in a smooth season.* "The LORD roars from Zion, and utters his voice from Jerusalem" Amos declares (1:2). "The LORD GOD has spoken; who can but prophesy?" he asks (3:8).

Now the book of Amos is small in comparison to the major writing prophets of the Old Testament (Isaiah, Jeremiah, and Ezekiel). Only nine chapters long, the contents of the book suggest that Amos's sermons were relatively short and self-contained. His ministry may have lasted only months and certainly no longer than a year or two. He probably traveled the circuit between Samaria, the capital of Israel, and the major religious centers of Bethel and Gilgal. Although Amos certainly came to the attention of the prophetic establishment and royal officials who considered him an agitator (chap. 7), nothing within the book suggests that any harm came to him. Rather, we may assume that after delivering the word of Yahweh for a season, this trailblazing prophet returned to his sheep and grove in Tekoa.

Our Text

Our text consists of what must have been Amos's most famous sermon. Every preacher would love to think that he or she had preached one sermon in his or her life this dramatic and powerful. It repays a careful study quite generously. This sermon is as important for its style and method of presentation as it is for its contents. It is, indeed, full of drama. We can be sure that whatever crowd may have gathered to hear this strange preacher on that day long ago got more than they bargained for—much more.

Let me try to set the scene. Amos—the "fig-pinching, sheep-poker," country preacher from Tekoa—has come to town. He is not exactly the type of preacher who is likely to get a spur-of-the-moment invitation to preach at the First Church, or any other church for that matter. His pulpit is the public square, the gate of the city, or the grounds outside the worship center where he might hope to draw a crowd. He is a street preacher, if you will, the kind that most dignified religious folk like you and me would not give much attention except as a curiosity or source of entertainment.

Yet, Amos has a sermon to deliver. God gave him a simple message, but it would not be easy to get a hearing. He knew that somehow he had to break through to his audience. Much was at stake. He was God's spokesperson for this moment. But how do you get through to people who are enjoying enormous prosperity? How do you get an audience to listen to harsh words in a smooth season? Unless the people of Israel heard Yahweh's message and responded appropriately, Amos could see the handwriting on the wall for the small kingdom of Israel—and it did not look good.

Of course, we have no way of knowing how big the crowd was for this dramatic sermon. Somehow I would like to think Amos drew a large group. The sermon can only be described as his homiletical masterpiece. Let us listen in and try to imagine ourselves in the crowd. I suspect the crowd was relatively small when Amos began preaching that day. Perhaps a few people walking by stopped when they heard what they thought was the topic of the sermon.

Without any fancy introduction, Amos jumped right in. There was no time to waste. "This is what Yahweh has said: For three transgressions of Damascus,,and for four, I will not revoke the punishment" (1:3). That statement probably caught some people's attention. After all, Damascus was the capital of Syria (Aram), Israel's important and powerful neighbor to the northeast. There was no love lost between Israel and Syria. Syria was the chief adversary of Israel during countless border wars and skirmishes. What was this strange preacher going to say about Damascus? This might be worth a few minutes after all.

Amos recalled a barbarous act of war that was probably still fresh on the minds of his audience (2 Kgs 13:3-7).

> Because they have threshed Gilead with threshing sledges of iron. So I will send fire on the house of Hazael (a king) . . . I will break the gate bars of Damascus, and cut off the inhabitants . . . , and the people of Aram shall go into exile to Kir, says the LORD. (1:3b-5)

You could probably have heard a few amens after the first point of Amos's sermon. Probably others joined the crowd. Amos was at least entertaining. "Hey, stop and listen to this guy," a few in the crowd probably said to others passing by. It is always fun to hear about the dirty linens of one's neighbors. Everyone would agree that Damascus deserved whatever it received.

Amos's next point is no less dramatic. This time, however, he jumps to the southwest and delivers a blow to Israel's mortal enemies, the Philistines. Four of the five Philistine cities are singled out: "This is what Yahweh has said: For three transgressions of Gaza, and for four, I will not revoke the punishment; because they carried into exiles entire communities, to hand them over to Edom" (1:6).

Now Amos was cooking. The crowd was getting larger. We can almost overhear one onlooker say to another, "He's letting them have it now." Amos concluded that Gaza's despicable act of handing over the entire population of an area into exile would come back upon those people. "I will turn my hand against Ekron, and the remnant of the Philistines shall perish, says the LORD GOD" (1:8b).

Next Amos turned north again to the coastal area of the Phoenicians and their capital of Tyre. "This is what Yahweh has said:

> For three transgressions of Tyre, and for four I will not revoke the punishment; because they delivered entire communities to Edom and did not remember the covenant of kinship. So I will send a fire on the wall of Tyre, fire that shall devour its strongholds. (1:9-10)

The sin of Tyre was similar to that of the Phoenician cities. Tyre had broken a covenant of brotherhood with some other city or state (cf. 1 Kgs 5:12; 9:13; 16:29ff.).

By now it was obvious to anyone who was listening carefully. Amos had traveled from the northeast to the southwest and back to the northwest. He was singling out Israel's neighbors one by one. This was a great sermon—no pain for the audience. Who would he turn to next? By now he probably had his crowd in the palm of his hand. The listeners were hanging on to every word. They did not hear enough of this kind of preaching. And he had not even been preaching five minutes yet! "Let 'em have it Amos." The crowd was with him, and he knew it. Amos continued.

"This is what Yahweh has said:

> For three transgressions of Edom (southeast) and for four, I will not revoke the punishment; because he pursued his brother with the sword and cast off all pity; he maintained his anger perpetually, and kept his wrath forever. For three transgressions of the Ammonites (north of Edom), and for four, I will not revoke the punishment. For three transgressions of Moab (immediately north of Edom), and for four, I will not revoke the punishment. (1:11-15; 2:1-3)

If you had a map of the ancient Near Eastern world, you would clearly see that Amos is dealing with Israel's neighbors to the east. With one exception he has completely encircled Israel. Was the sermon over?

It had been a good ride. Amos had not left any enemy out. No patriotic Israelite could have helped but love the sermon preached by that southern, upstart, backwoods preacher. He had been on target, if not eloquent, to this point. But it was not over yet.

Probably almost without missing a beat, Amos began his next point. "This is what Yahweh has said: For three transgressions of Judah, and for four, I will not revoke the punishment" (2:4-5). Amos had saved the best for last—or so they thought. Now he was about to come down on the southern kingdom of Judah. What a climax! This preacher is all right! He was going to come down hard on his own people now. Few people in the crowd would not have enjoyed a thorough condemnation of their brothers and sisters in the South. The northern kingdom of Israel had lived in the shadows of Judah and its Davidic monarchy ever since the country broke apart some 175 years before in 922 B.C. following the death of Solomon.

So Amos began his next point. The people of Judah had rejected the law of Yahweh; they had abandoned God's statutes. "They have been led astray by the same lies after which their ancestors walked. So I will send a fire on Judah, and it shall devour the strongholds of Jerusalem" (2:4b). Even mighty Jerusalem, where Yahweh's presence resided in the temple, could not withstand the judgment of Yahweh that was certain when God's people forsake God's sacred law.

The people probably responded to this indictment in at least two ways. Some would have certainly signaled their approval with sneers, laughter, and amens. They would have been happy to hear anyone speak of Yahweh's disapproval of Judah. Israel and Judah were for the most part jealous siblings. Most of Amos's crowd would have thought that Judah was getting exactly what the nation deserved.

On a deeper level, however, some folks in the crowd long ago might have gained some respect for this prophet as a result of this sermon. After all, Amos was from the South. He worked and lived only about ten miles from Jerusalem. The very fact that he spoke difficult words concerning his own people reflected the seriousness of this prophet's message. Maybe Amos was more than an entertaining street preacher after all.

By now Amos's sermon was almost over. The crowd had been on a rollercoaster ride of delight. Amos held both the respect and the attention of his audience however large or small it was. Yet, nothing could have prepared his hearers for what came next. Having encircled Israel as Amos clicked off its neighbors one by one, now came the real sermon—the part that was hard to hear, but the part for this audience that made all the difference in the world. No, the sermon was not over; one more point was to be made.

"This is what Yahweh has said:

> For three transgressions of Israel, and for four, I will not revoke the punishment; because they sell the righteous for silver, and the needy for a pair of sandals—they who trample the head of the poor into the dust of the earth, and push the afflicted out of the way; father and son go in to the same girl, so that my holy name is profaned; they lay themselves down beside every altar on garments taken in pledge; and in the house of God they drink wine bought with fines they imposed. (2:6-8)

You could have heard a pin drop. Amos had now made the time-honored transition from preaching to meddling. He was hitting too close to home. Who is this upstart country preacher to come up here and tell us what's wrong with Israel? the people may have muttered. Yet, in these moments, Amos was fulfilling his calling. His message had been delivered. The hardest but best sermon Amos ever preached had fallen upon the ears of his audience in less than ten minutes. He spoke the truth. He proclaimed the Yahweh word. "Is it not indeed so?" he asked the people of Israel. Who could challenge his words that rang so true? In the quietness of shock and truth, Amos's words demanded a response. Now it was up to them. How would they respond?

What Do We Do with This?

The truth is we do not know how Amos's audience responded to his sermon. We do know, however, that Israel fell to the Assyrians in 722 B.C. The historians and prophets of the Old Testament had no problems in interpreting those historic events as the punishment of Yahweh upon the people of Israel because they had forgotten that relationship to God means not only privilege, but responsibility.

Perhaps the most important question today is not about ancient Israel, but about us. What could these words of an eighth-century prophet have to do with us? Is this simply an interesting tale about a curious preacher and a dramatic sermon? As a student of the Old Testament, I confess I often struggle with these questions. It is difficult to find relevance and a word from God that transcends the years.

Here, however, in Amos's famous sermon I find something that disturbs me more than I would ordinarily care to admit. If nothing else, Amos was convinced that a nation's worth in the eyes of God is determined by the way it relates to those in need. Did you hear that? A nation's worth in the eyes of God is determined by the way it relates to those in need. Israel and Judah, along with all the other nations, were judged by God as a result of actions taken against people—people in need, sometimes relatives, sometimes people who were helpless in those ancient societies—be they the casualties of barbarous wars, pregnant women, or simply as in Israel's case the righteous who were worth no more to the nation than the price of a pair of shoes; or the poor who are trampled into the face of the earth and the afflicted who are pushed out of the way in that never-ceasing struggle for power, dominance, wealth, and resources with which the history of this planet is colored.

When it is all boiled down, it has to do with that greatest and most dastardly of human sin: the self-centeredness that possesses us both individually and corporately, which has within it the power to crush the human soul and keep us from becoming before God who we were created to become. Rather, in our turning inward, we become less than we are and reject the greatest thing about ourselves: our capacities for relationship with God and love of neighbor.

In our own country, which has been so blessed, we find ourselves in the midst of a political revolution. Regardless of which side one may take, no one could argue that it has not been fascinating to watch. The watchword of the hour is a balanced budget. No one could argue against these efforts. We all know they are necessary. The waste and abuse of Washington are legendary. Yet, I cannot help but wonder what it says about our own country when we watch the debates and consider the priorities that our nation embraces.

What would Amos say about our nation—indeed, our city, our religious community—if he were to preach his sermon in front of city hall today? I think he would tell us that God would rather we feed a hungry child than buy one more bullet or weapon than we absolutely need. I think he would tell us that God would rather we educate a child than pay for a politician to ride around in a limousine for another day. I think he would tell us that God would rather we give needy people a hand and help them to provide for themselves and become responsible citizens than doom another generation to the cruel cycle of poverty. And I think he would say that God would rather we invest in care for the elderly and provide basic affordable health care for those to whom we owe so much than to spend another dollar on useless and costly government waste.

Amos would remind us that a nation's worth in the eyes of God is determined by the way it relates to those in need. Of course, Amos was shocked that Israel, a nation that enjoyed a special relationship to Yahweh, could do the things that the nation stood accused of. Amos reminded the people of what Yahweh had done for them. "I brought you up out of the land of Egypt, and led you forty years in the wilderness, to possess the land . . . I raised up some of your children to be prophets" (2:10-11). God expects more of God's people. For Israel, relationship with God had become a privilege, but Israel forgot about the responsibility. Amos concluded with a question, "Is it not indeed so, O people of Israel?" (2:11).

What about God's people today? What would go before Amos's question today? "Is it not indeed so?" Just as Israel stood on the other side of the great Old Testament salvific event—the Exodus from Egypt—so we live on the other side of the second great salvific event of the Bible—the cross. Yet the church today is so often preoccupied with everything except that for which it was born. So today sociologists and historians speak about the irrelevancy and demise of Christianity. Ministers are burned out and leaving the ministry. Fewer students are preparing for the ministry. The most successful churches in attracting Baby Boomers and Generation X are those that replace entertainment for worship or a neat black-and-white system of belief that leads congregations and individuals to turn inward closing out the world—all those who do not pass their particular litmus tests of faith.

Although it would be easier to focus on the sins of our neighbors, the church would do well to look at its own sins. We would do well to look at *our* own sins. The author of 1 John had a simple view of what the life of faith is all about: "For this is the message you have heard from the beginning, that we should love one another" (3:11). But he did not see this love in the abstract. Like Amos, the author of 1 John knew that relationship with God impacts the way we live out our lives in the everydayness of life. So he asked,

> How does God's love abide in anyone who has the world's goods and sees a brother or sister in need and yet refuses help? Little children, let us love, not in word or speech, but in truth and action. (vv. 17-18)

I tell you my friends, we are not the church, and we are not the people of God until we live out that love. I tell you the darkness of this world will not be won to the light of Christ until what we say we believe becomes what we do, until what we do in here as church becomes what we do out there as church in the world. Is it not indeed so, O Israel? asked Amos of the people of Israel long ago. Is it not indeed so, O people of God! Amen.

Note

[1]For further information on cities referenced in Amos 1:3–2:16, see appropriate articles in the *Mercer Dictionary of the Bible* (Macon GA: Mercer University Press, 1990).

[2]Quoting Biddle, see page 5.

Chapter Three

On Walking with God

Amos 3

William L. Coates, Jr.

Background

Chapters 3–6 comprise the central unit of the book of Amos and contain the central thought of Amos's prophecy to Israel. Verses 1 and 2 of chapter 3 provide the opening statement for this unit and establish the theme that dominates all of chapters 3–6. Though Amos was, in his words, "no prophet nor the son of a prophet" (meaning that he was not a "preacher" by profession but was called to deliver a specific message to a specific people in their specific situation), he certainly uses the approach of a well-trained modern minister. He distills his "sermon" down to one sentence and uses this sentence as the thematic statement right at the beginning. The listener or reader knows from the start what the sermon is about.

3:1-2. Amos warns of coming judgment. "Hear this word" is a command, an imperative to be obeyed, indicating that what follows is not to be taken lightly. Further, it is the word "that the LORD has spoken," thus strengthening the imperative and fortifying the authority of the speaker himself. This is not mere talk or opinion or an idea from just anyone; it is the authoritative statement of reality uttered by Yahweh, the Creator, the same one whose spoken word first brought the creation to order. This time, however, Yahweh's word will bring disorder and destruction, for it is spoken "against" Israel. The Creator

God, the God of the covenant, will now move, not to build up, but to tear down.

This warning is not limited to the northern kingdom of Israel, but is meant for the whole nation, both Israel and the southern kingdom of Judah, for it is "spoken against you, O people of Israel, against the whole family." This message would prove to be correct and this prophet's words justified, particularly in the case of Israel, which would be obliterated, virtually wiped off the map, in 722 B.C. by the Assyrians. Judah, though later under Cyrus of Persia allowed to rebuild as the new nation of Israel, would be destroyed by the Babylonians in 587/6 B.C.

Amos, while speaking to Israel, was himself from Judah and clearly saw the sinful situation in both kingdoms as being about equal: idolatrous, selfish, oppressive, and very religious outwardly while inwardly spiritually perverse. So the sermon is a jeremiad, or lamentation or complaint, directed "against the whole family that I brought up out of the land of Egypt." God will now bring down what God had previously brought up.

Verse 2 is striking. God says through Amos what God had said through Moses: "You only have I known of all the families of the earth." This statement is a reference to God's election of Israel as the instrument through which God would accomplish God's work and make known the divine purpose. This phrase usually precedes a statement of the people's great responsibility and God's great outpouring of blessing upon them, but the "therefore" is now followed by the harsh announcement: "I will punish you for all your iniquities."

Note that the word is not "sins" (which would mean "missing the mark," failing to live up to potential), nor is it "transgressions" (which would mean "rebellion" or "violation of the law"). The word is "iniquities"—"crookedness" or "deceit." Of the three words that denote types of sins, iniquities is the worst, for it indicates evil so entrenched that it no longer is able to make distinctions between right and wrong. The tone is ominous, for such wicked reality is surely to meet the worst kind of opposition and punishment. Being chosen had its privileges but also its demands, and not fulfilling the demands would have severe consequences.

3:3-6. Now that the message is introduced, the focus shifts from the pronouncement of God to a series of questions by Amos, each of them designed to demonstrate action and reponse, or cause and effect. According to verse 3, two persons must agree (literally "meet") in order to walk together. They must set the time to meet and begin their walk, and they must share in purpose and destination. Without agreement they can only go separately. Just so, God and Israel have to part ways since they no longer agree.

Verses 4-6 contain parallel questions. The lion roars for a reason. The bird is trapped because a snare has been set. The people in the city fear because a trumpet of warning has been sounded. Things happen because something causes them. In the same way, the calamity that will come upon the city will be the result of a cause: The Lord will have done it. The coming disaster will be the result of previous decisions and actions. Israel will undergo tumultuous and horrifying events, and these will not be a quirk of history or a sad situation with no explanation or reason. They will, in fact, be the direct result of Israel's straying from their walk, their agreement, with God. The values of Israel no longer meet with the will of the Sovereign Lord. The effect of this lack of meeting will be national upheaval.

3:7-8. Amos now follows his questions with a statement verifying his authority to ask them. Even in judgment God is still fulfilling the divine role in the covenant by making God's plans known through the prophet. The prophet's listening ear hears God's "secret" revealed, and the prophet interprets its meaning. The roar of the lion is a metaphor for God's wrath against the chosen people, all of whom will fear when they too hear it. They will be in awe just as the prophet himself is upon hearing the horror in God's announcement.

3:9-15. These seven verses begin to delineate the specifics of the nation's evil. First, Amos speaks of Samaria, the political center of Israel. Foreign powers are called upon to witness the awful state of affairs in the nation. Many scholars agree that Ashdod, a city of Philistia, may not be the intended reading here in verse 9, so they follow the Septuagint reading, which is "Assyria." Such a reading does seem more reasonable in the context, for Assyria and Egypt were both powers that bordered Israel. By implication, these nations that do not even know Yahweh will be embarrassed as they observe God's own people in action.

Israel is described as a people who do not even know what is right from wrong and as ones who do not only commit violence and robbery, or destruction, but actually "store up" such acts and fill their palaces with it. This could mean that they pile one destructive work upon another, or it could be saying that their actions will have the effect of storing up the inevitable destruction that awaits them.

"Therefore," God pronounces that an enemy shall invade and empty the palaces and rob the robbers. The destruction will be so thorough that Amos uses a graphic simile to depict it. If a sheep were missing from the owner's flock due to a lion's attack, apparently the shepherd would have to produce evidence that such had occurred, such as "two legs or a piece of an ear." In the same way, all the wealthy Samarians would soon have to show would be "the corner of a couch" or "part of a bed."

Now, in verses 13 and 14, the prophet addresses the religious life of Israel. "Hear and testify" are words of the courtroom, as if witnesses are being called for the prosecution of Israel ("house of Jacob"). The prosecutors are to present their case that Israel has broken the covenant arrangement with God. Here he speaks of Israel's "transgressions," or outright rebellions, against Yahweh's authority. This is surely aimed at the Baal worship and religious syncretism so prevalent during Jeroboam II's long reign.

Israel, with no defense, will be found guilty of gross idolatry, resulting in the destruction of "the altars of Bethel." Bethel is the sacred place where Jacob had wrestled with the angel and was the site of the royal sanctuary, the chief center of worship for Israel. The place of worship would not be exempt from the coming destruction. Even "the horns of the altar shall be cut off and fall to the ground." This statement indicates that no place of refuge or safety would exist for the people, for the horns of the altar had traditionally been the place of safe escape in the sanctuary.

Finally, in verse 15 and continuing into the beginning of chapter 4, Amos indicts the national culture, particularly that represented by the uncaring wealthy class. God will "tear down the winter houses as well as the summer houses" and the ivory-laden mansions and the "great houses," possibly a reference to the great holdings of real estate that some possessed. This indictment continues in the next chapter as the crushed needy and the oppressed poor are specifically discussed. The inference here is that God's punishment of Israel is all the more justified, because not only has Israel failed the terms of the covenant in not caring to convey the truth of God to other nations, but Israel has failed to care even for its own people, fellow members of the covenant community.

A word about context: The words of Amos must surely have seemed incredulous to the people to whom they were spoken. This was a time when, on the surface, all appears to have been going well. During the long reign of Jeroboam II, Israel lived in a window of opportunity and prosperity. Those with wealth saw their wealth increase vastly. The nation's enemies were too busy in other campaigns that did not involve them, so there was relative independence and peace. The houses of worship were filled with worshipers every Sabbath. It was one of the brighter periods of the nation's history, and the Deuteronomic theology taught Israel that God blessed those who were faithful and cursed those who were not. Thus, these indictments and words of doom in chapter 3 must have seemed all the more unbelievable.

Application for Preaching and Teaching

On Walking with God
Amos 3

Certain phrases go together, or at least they have almost proverb-like status. Consider, for example: "Like father, like son." "As the twig is bent, so grows the tree." "If you want to have a friend, you must be a friend." Some statements, once begun, have logical and expected conclusions, endings so sure they all but require a "therefore": "You are my best friend; therefore I can tell you this in confidence." "You are the one I love; therefore I want you to marry me." "You are doing a great job; therefore you are getting a promotion." So, complete this sentence: "You only have I known of all the families of the earth; therefore. . . . "

Therefore I will honor you especially? Therefore I will give you that which I offer to no other? Therefore I will protect and defend you?

Now look at Amos 3:2 and get a great surprise. God says to Israel, "You only have I known of all the families of the earth, therefore *I will punish you for all your iniquities.*" This has to be one of the great ironic statements in all of scripture. I have known you and formed a unique relationship with you; therefore I am getting ready to destroy you? What's going on here?

Yes, God had a unique relationship with Israel. God had known the Israelites, even chosen them and brought them out of bondage. What a privilege! God had bestowed upon these people a singular blessing. It appears, however, that Israel had come to expect that entitlement and blessing were the only reasons for which they had been chosen. There seemed to be no sense of obligation. But a good relationship, by its very nature, must have both privilege and responsibility.

Amos expounds upon this idea of relationship with a question: "Do two walk together unless they have made an appointment?" Can there be a meaningful relationship unless there is a meeting of the minds, or a consensus of purpose, or a joining of wills? God had indeed called Israel to walk with God, but the calling had meant exactly that—to walk *with* God. To walk with God is a high privilege. To walk without God—to walk alone or with other company—is to walk irresponsibly and without God's benefits. Amos's preaching gives clear warning of this. He was speaking, of course, to an entire nation that had forsaken its covenant of walking with God.

Israel had gone its way alone, and worse, the nation had even chosen to keep company with any number of gods. During Jeroboam II's long reign, and prior to that, the people had forgotten their allegiance to Yahweh who had "brought [them] up out of the land of Egypt" and had worshiped the baals of Canaanite culture and had trusted in military alliances with foreign powers. Many of the Israelites had also made wealth and material goods their top priority. In their beginning days of enslavement in Egypt, they had walked, however feebly, with God to their liberation and identity as the covenant people. Now, in the long season of prosperity and relative independence, they had chosen to take the dangerous walk without God. Therefore, God will punish.

In reality, punishment was inevitable, even inherent. It was not so much an act of God as it was a natural result of not walking with God. After all, the benefits of walking with God are not possible if one chooses to walk alone or to walk with another. This reality was not limited to Amos's day or to Israel's situation. The privilege and the responsibility of relationship with God, as well as the inherent punishment of walking without God, are equally as true today. What, then, does it mean to walk with God? Walking with God means first meeting with God. Two people have to get together before they can be together.

A couple of years ago, I was to meet a friend at a restaurant for dinner. I arrived on time and sat down in the lobby to wait for him. After what seemed to me an eternity, I asked the hostess, for the second time, if she had seen or heard anything from my friend. She said she had not, but perhaps I would like to walk around inside and see if, by any chance, he was present. I did and he was. He had arrived a short time before me and had asked to be seated for a cup of coffee. For fifty minutes he and I had been in the same building and were separated by a thin wall, even though the space between us was no more than twenty feet. We could have been together all that time, enjoying a conversation, but we were not because we had not met together.

How much of your average day is lived alone or in poor company because you did not first meet with God? How much of your life is lived this way? I want the benefit of God's company, wisdom, and presence. I do not want my life punished by God's absence. Reason and experience, not to mention scripture, tell me that to have the effect, I must have the cause; to walk in God's company, I must meet with God first. Personally, I like an appointment with God early each day.

Walking with God also means agreeing with God. There has to be a meeting, but there also has to be a meeting of the minds. If two people cannot walk together harmoniously, the time will not be well-spent nor will it have a good ending. Relationships that are healthy and life-affirming are built on agreement, and agreements are matters of choice. Relationship with God is a choice, an act of the will. Though it is initiated by God's grace, the individual must choose whether to respond.

I like the words of the traditional Episcopal marriage ceremony, particularly the first set of vows. The words are not, "*Do* you take this woman to be your wife or this man to be your husband?" Rather, they are "*Will* you take this woman to be your wedded wife, to live together after God's ordinance in the holy estate of matrimony? Will you love her, honor and keep her in sickness and in health, to love and to cherish, til death do you part?" The word *will* indicates a commitment that is intended to be kept for the future, not simply a feeling to enjoy for the present. That will is the basis for an agreement, a covenant, that has the potential to bless and benefit both parties for life. Likewise, a covenant with God is an agreement that has life-giving benefits.

Walking with God implies traveling at the same pace. I have noticed that many married couples have difficulty walking together. One is a fast-paced walker, while the other is a mere stroller. One couple I observed in a mall were clearly out of sync. Walking briskly and facing straight ahead, he was carrying on quite a conversation with his no-longer-existent partner. She had dropped back to a vastly reduced pace about twelve stores ago, all the while looking ahead mischievously to see the reaction when he finally would catch on.

A great contrast is evident in Amos 3. The prophet is calling the nation to walk *with* God but all the while is sounding the clear warning that, because of the present circumstances, God is *against* the chosen people. Their pace was not the same. God preferred the slow walk of intimacy, while Israel was on the frantic treadmill of progress and prosperity. While God wanted quality and depth of relationship, Israel was running ahead for quantity and increase of goods. Walking with God means movement toward a common destination, having the sense of going somewhere together, even if it is not so much a place as a condition that is the goal.

I remember a hymn that the choir in my little rural home church used to sing. The words are folksy and sentimental, but they present the image of two persons walking together in mutuality.

> My God and I go in the fields together,
> We walk and talk as good friends should and do.
> We clasp our hands, our voices ring with laughter,
> My God and I walk through the meadow's hue.[1]

God is interested in certain things, love and justice being chief among them. Anyone who walks with God has to walk in pursuit of these same goals. But Israel is characterized as a people of oppression and selfishness whose winter and summer houses "and the houses of ivory shall perish, and the great houses shall come to an end" (3:15). While God was walking one path, moving toward the redemption of all people through God's chosen nation, Israel had clearly chosen another. In fact, Amos actually calls for foreign neighbors to "assemble on Mount Samaria" and take a look at the road Israel had chosen, a road with an entirely opposite destination than any place God would have led them. Even foreigners would be disgusted with Israel's oppression and selfishness, for "they do not know how to do right" and they "store up violence and robbery." God and Israel could not walk together because they were not going the same way.

The message of Amos is hard to hear. I would rather listen to John saying "The law was indeed given through Moses; but grace and truth came through Jesus Christ" (John 1:17). The words of Amos contain little grace, but plenty of judgment. There are dire predictions of punishment, even graphic ones. When God is through with Israel, says Amos, only the corner of a couch or a piece of a bed will be left. Even the altar in the house of worship will be destroyed. Amos was right. Some time later Israel was virtually obliterated in a war with Assyria.

We do not have many prophets among us today, and the few who do cry out warnings to the church in our century, people such as Carlyle Marney, have results similar to those of Amos. They do not get much of an audience. We want to hear words of comfort and affirmation, not words of challenge and change. We desire the privilege of walking with God without having to follow the demands God makes upon us on the way. It is nice to hear that we are chosen, but what is the "therefore" that comes after?

Are God and the church agreed? Are God and you in agreement? Two can walk together if they are agreed. Genesis 5:24 reads, "Enoch walked with God; then he was no more, because God took him." After reading this verse in Sunday School one day, a little girl was asked what her class had learned that morning. She told her version: "One day God and Enoch went out for a walk. They were enjoying each other so much that they walked a long, long way. They walked so long that finally it began to get dark. And they had walked so far that God turned to Enoch and said, 'Enoch, it's closer to my house than it is to yours, so why don't you just come on home with me?' "

Note

[1]"My God and I," Austris A. Wihtol, 1935.

Chapter Four

Now Hear This!

Amos 4

James M. Pitts

Structure

Within chapter 4 we find an exhortation (vv. 1-5), statements about disaster (vv. 6-11), a threatening speech (v. 12), and a hymn (v. 13). This section of scripture presents a recitation of excessive luxury, sinful piety, and ignored warnings. The exhortation opens with "Hear this . . ." A statement about disaster follows. It cascades from famine, drought, blight and locusts, plague and war, and fire. Then a threat to Israel is made, warning the people to prepare to meet their God. A hymn marks the end of chapter 4 and concludes the pronouncements of doom.

Amos's vocation as a shepherd and "dresser of sycamore trees" was disrupted by God's call to be a prophet. Living beyond the power line of privilege and prestige in Tekoa, a village southeast of Bethlehem, Amos received a call to be a prophet that involved both surprise and dreadful responsibility. His mission was not to predict but to exhort, announce judgment, and persuade.

The book of Amos, which covers approximately eight pages, can be read in fifteen to twenty minutes. Yet, this succinct message has informed the faithful and intrigued scholars over generations. The contemporary situation prompting Amos's concern was oppression and corruption in commerce and courtrooms. The people were guilty of crimes against humanity. They were complacent, bloated with pride, floating on a wave of economic prosperity, and religiously arrogant. Military successes insulated the people from God and justice.

In this high time of power and prosperity, the people of pride and plenty were blind to the downside and stress of success. The words of the prophets were resisted and dismissed. The people were oblivious to any threat by outside forces, such as Assyria or Egypt. Destruction or domination of Israel was not a part of their perceptual forecast. The early warning system of prophetic discernment went unheeded.

4:1-3 presents an attack on the nobility of Samaria. A particular condemnation is made of the women. In their addiction to wine, they are compared to the fat cows of Bashan. Because of their unquenchable thirst for luxury and leisure, the rich oppress the poor and crush the needy. In their covetous demands for more, they are oblivious and indifferent to human rights. While the privileged have all they need, yet want more, the poor are sinking into misery. While the spotlight is on Samaria, the prophet's message is a floodlight addressing the whole nation of two kingdoms, north and south. Exile is promised as their punishment. Defeat, destruction, and death await them. Like cattle led to slaughter, their carcasses will be dragged to judgment.

4:4-5 serves as a transition for the upcoming pronouncement of plagues. The cultic centers of Bethel and Gilgal are named. Later, in Amos's prophetic judgment, the name of Beersheba will be added. All were centers of religious pilgrimage commemorating the exodus from Egypt and settlement of the land. Because of their historical ties, they were regarded as national shrines. Bethel represented the royal establishment. Its worship services were the dream of a chamber of commerce.

The shrines' accommodating attitude and inclusion of other deities prompted by practical and economic reasons were a prophet's nightmare. There is no substitute for God. Apostasy and idolatry are beyond the bounds of acceptable worship and an abomination to prophetic expectations. Later (5:21-24) Amos will declare that the destruction of Bethel will not be a tragedy in the nation's religious life, but a triumph. Bethel, from the prophetic perspective, represented a spiritual flaw in the spiritual character of the people. Their self-centered focus in worship illustrated what was fundamentally wrong in Israel's relationship with God. Elaborate ceremony is no substitute for just conduct. Righteousness is desired more than ritual.

4:6-12 offers a refrain of the opening oracles against the nations (1:1–2:8). In this section, the grouping of the plagues expresses that they were sent by God to warn of an impending judgment and to encourage the people to repentance. The people are invited to reverse their direction and be saved from disaster. Together, the plagues form an indescribable destruction and inconceivable catastrophe. The destructive plagues were sent to achieve a constructive purpose. Beyond the dreadful damage, the desired hope was that repentance would occur. A saving encounter was anticipated. This did not happen. Although they were distressed, injured, and overwhelmed, the people "did not return to God."

The same God who had formed the Israelites as a nation and led them to the land of promise, would now destroy and devastate God's own people and remove them from the land. This was a new, shocking, and completely incomprehensible scenario to Amos's hearers. No one had said anything like this to them before. So, of course, it could not be true. For Amos, judgment was not arbitrary, capricious, or unfeeling. The Sovereign Lord who brought the Isralites from Egypt and gave them the land also told them how to live in this land. They were warned by the prophets about the consequences of not living up to the standards set for them. Yet, they dismissed the prophetic warning and guiding pronouncements. The prophets were silenced and dismissed. Only the inevitability of judgment remained.

Representing either the signature of the prophet himself or an early commentator, each utterance describing a calamity concludes, "Yet you did not return to me, says the LORD." The plagues were a prophetic counterpoint. They were a warning and a sign of things to come. Each plague was a punishment and a plea exhorting the people to change their ways. The objective was repentance. Instead of the plagues prompting a return to God, the people continued to resist and reject God's pleading to return. The message of both prophets and plagues to repent and return was rejected. In these verses the prophetic rationale for judgment is offered.

The plagues follow the literary device of treaty discourses in Deuteronomy 28–29 and Leviticus 26. Also, they reflect the plague tradition of the Exodus story. So, here in Amos, we find an echo of both the history of literary transmission and the actuality of human experience. The epidemic of plagues seems to multiply, spread, and build on each other.

In the list famine is first, followed by drought. Generally, drought precedes famine. The third combines blight, mildew, and locusts. Together they intensify the famine and thwart efforts at recovery. The fourth plague combines the twin offspring of war, disease, and defeat. Many armies have experienced defeat by disease before they encountered their mortal enemy on the field of battle. The fifth plague references Sodom and Gomorrah. These ancient cities present a popular prophetic symbol of destruction by fire. Like a "fire from heaven," there will be a shaking of foundations, and a firestorm will inhale and incinerate—generating complete destruction. Yet, a spark of hope is seized in the ashes. The phrase, "You were like a brand snatched from the fire," is pregnant with possibility. A similar phrase appears in Zechariah 3:2, referring to Joshua.

Out of the current crisis and conflagration, a brand not completely consumed is spared. Out of the ashes of the rubble and ruin, something small and seemingly insignificant is retrieved. Yet, all of these efforts to redeem meet with failure. In mournful despair, the prophet conveys the disappointment of a brokenhearted God. "Yet you did not return to me, says the LORD" (v. 11d).

All of these efforts were futile. The experiment with repentance through plague failed miserably and was abandoned. Hunger, drought, blight, locusts, pestilence, slaying of sons, and destruction of cities had no effect. What then? No longer will calls to repentance be issued. The people are summoned to a divine settlement. With their refusal to listen and learn, the people could only "prepare to meet your God," as verse 12 states. There would be no more invitations to repent. The next item on the divine/human agenda is neither prophetic pleading nor plague. All that remains is devastating judgment. Having ignored the Lord's repeated warnings through nature and history, God will meet them. "Prepare to meet your God, O Israel."

4:13 is a cosmic hymn. It is a reminder to all persons of the identity of Yahweh, the God of Israel. In a world filled with tribal deities and surrounded by patron and partisan gods, the God of Israel stands supreme and alone. Yahweh is not one among many or the leader of the pack. Yahweh is not a minor god of a minuscule nation, like a plush cat on a carnival rack, a prize in the pantheon. The size of the nation Israel had nothing to do with the scope and power of its God. Yahweh is the creator and sustainer of the world and all that is. Yahweh has no rivals. Yahweh is dependent on nothing and no one. To God belongs all power and authority.

The phrase or doxology of the God who speaks is a refrain that also concludes the Book of Woes (6:14) and the Book of Visions (9:6). God will not leave humanity in the dark. At the end of the tunnel is the light of the earth-maker, pain-bearer, and life-giver. Through the intimacy of the prophet's relationship with God and his understanding of God's thoughts and purposes, God's intentions are declared to humanity. God is coming to set things right.

Application for Preaching and Teaching

Now Hear This!
Amos 4:1-13

During recent days in Savannah, Georgia, much attention has been given to "the book." I am not referring to the Bible, but to *Midnight in the Garden of Good and Evil.* For over a year, John Berendt's bestseller has caught the public's attention. In an imaginative manner, it recounts the beautiful and bizarre, the mossy wonder and voodoo weirdness of a coastal southern city. The poster of the city portrayed in the book brings a smile to promoters of tourism. Others, the preservers of tradition and protectors of place, see the book as a caricature. For the cultured ladies and gentlemen of society, this fiction is unworthy and the subject of private disdain and open disgust. From the discerning eye of an outsider, Savannah is described as class-conscious and gossipy, mannered and moneyed, and soaked to its soul in the finest of distilled spirits.

One can only imagine the scorn that would be heaped upon the prophet Amos if he were to come and observe, speak, and write about Savannah or our city. We are always eager to show folks the chamber of commerce's "better-side tour" of success and opportunity, wealth and culture. The welcome mat is out. We embrace with open arms any and all who will add to the financial bottom line. Social critics and out-siders, investigative reporters, do-gooders and disturbers of the status quo, and certainly God-intoxicated visionaries and spiritual fellow trav-elers are not welcome. Go away! Stay away! Keep your opinions to yourself!

To the folks living it up in the northern kingdom of Israel, Amos was an uninvited, unexpected, and unwelcome intruder. He was liter-ally a nobody from nowhere. His address was a rural route beyond the power line of society, some six miles south from the breadbasket town of Bethlehem. Amos's Tekoa was on the edge of the desert, a marginal place in the semi-barren hills of Judea's eastern watershed.

The residents of Israel certainly did not send for him, but this shep-herd and pruner of sycamore blooms was sent. His simple rural life had been disrupted by a call from God. In a visit to Samaria, Amos was shocked by what he observed. Luxury existed in the midst of poverty, injustice was celebrated, the poor were oppressed, bribery was accepted, worship was self-serving and degenerate. What was good for me and mine and business was the greatest and only good. Their greatest need was simply for more.

Religion was popular with the wealthy. Many residents built second homes near the worship sites at Bethel and Dan. New shrines were con-structed at Gilgal and Beersheba. The rich assumed that their prosperity was a sign of God's blessing and approval. Yet, their religious devotion with its elaborate rituals did not inform their social concern or prompt compassion. They were brutally indifferent and insensitive to human need. To the prophetic perception, these good times of peace and prosperity were rotten to the core. Beneath the surface veneer of "looking good" was profound moral and spiritual depravity.

Without a formal theological education or technical training in the school of professional prophets, Amos spoke. Rejecting any con-nections with the religious enthusiasts and entrepreneurs, Amos spoke.

Responding to a sense of divine obligation, Amos spoke not as a self-serving promoter, but as a prophet, as a spokesperson for God. Amos did not speak as an eager volunteer pretending to help others while primarily helping himself. He spoke as a person who had been called and sent like an ambassador on a mission of ultimate importance. Amos joined a long line of unlikely candidates for ministry called and commissioned by God.

Later in the story of salvation, the apostle Paul will remind his contemporaries in faith of their marginal status.

> Consider your own call, brothers and sisters: not many of you were wise by human standards, not many were powerful, not many were of noble birth. But God chose what is foolish in the world to shame the wise; God chose what is weak in the world to shame the strong; God chose what is low and despised in the world, things that are not, to reduce to nothing things that are, so that no one might boast in the presence of God. He is the source of your life in Christ Jesus, who became for us wisdom from God, and righteousness and sanctification and redemption, in order that, as it is written, "Let the one who boasts, boast in the Lord." (1 Cor 1:26-31)

Against a background of material prosperity, inspired by God, Amos took a deep breath and spoke. Burdened with the moral and spiritual depravity of his people, Amos was not out to win friends. His mission was to exhort and persuade people to pay attention to the declarations and demands of God. He was an equal opportunity offender. Bold, simple, and direct, Amos spoke as a person with character and values shaped by an encounter with the Lord.

Now hear this. Amos begins with "a ladies first" pronouncement.

> Hear this word, you cows of Bashan who are on Mount Samaria, who oppress the poor, who crush the needy, who say to their husbands, "Bring something to drink!" The LORD GOD has sworn by his holiness: The time is surely coming upon you, when they shall take you away with hooks, even the last of you with fishhooks. Through

breaches in the wall you shall leave, each one straight ahead; and you
shall be flung out into Harmon, says the LORD. (4:1-3)

Amos's attack on the noble women of Bashan would be judged as politically incorrect, both then and now. Calling people fat cows, excessive
drinkers, selfish and socially insensitive is a rough and tough opening
shot. We need to remember that Amos was not a smooth political
operator, but a prophet speaking for God with candor and clarity.

From Amos's inspired perspective, the prosperity of the people
had insulated them from the harsh realities of life. Their channels of
perception did not receive the plight of the poor. They were indifferent
to human rights. In their demands for more, they could care less. Like
addicts of all ages, their denial system worked well. Their private security system prevented unwanted messages and unwelcome sights.
There was no personal connection, no heartfelt responsibility, no
glance of compassion. They were turned off to others and detached
from the larger world. Their focus was exclusively on self. Their insatiable thirst was for another drink. Like alcoholics of all ages, each
drink calls for another.

From the prophet's perspective their prognosis was poor, if not
awful. Exile is promised as punishment. Like cattle led to slaughter, the
bovines of Bashan would experience defeat, destruction, and death.
The carousers' party is coming to an end. Their destination is the city
dump and refuse heap of history.

To the people living in denial, the prophet continues to speak.
Now hear this . . .

Come to Bethel—and transgress; to Gilgal—and multiply transgression; bring your sacrifices every morning, your tithes every three
days; bring a thank-offering of leavened bread, and proclaim freewill
offerings, publish them; for so you love to do, O people of Israel! says
the LORD GOD. (vv. 4-5)

Amos had even less respect for the religious establishment than he had for the rich women. With sarcasm, Amos mocks a religious enterprise that had been perverted into a celebration of self-interest and a means for evading the commandments of God. The elaborate rituals became a point of rebellion. Pilgrimages, sacrifices, tithes, and offerings have become acts of transgression. The people loved religious ritual. It met their need for public recognition, power, and prestige. The problem was that in worship their focus had shifted away from God and toward self. They assembled to address their own selfish agendas and not to be addressed by God's agenda for them. True worship, in the prophetic perspective, acknowledges a connection between worship ceremonies and responding to God's demands for righteousness and justice.

Later in the faith story, following in the prophetic tradition and in response to a question regarding the priorities of life,

> Jesus answered . . . 'The first is, "Hear, O Israel: the Lord our God, the Lord is one; you shall love the Lord your God with all your heart, and with all your soul, and with all your mind, and with all your strength." The second is this, "You shall love your neighbor as yourself." There is no other commandment greater than these.' (Mark 12:29-31)

True religion is a seamless garment of faithfulness to God and responsibility to neighbor.

Jesus prefaced many of his remarks: "Let anyone with ears to hear listen!" (Mark 4:23). Like those who were deaf to the Lord, the patrons of religious life in Israel were not paying attention to Amos. They were ignoring God's ethical admonitions. Their lack of receptivity did not prevent Amos from continuing his words of judgment. Like an echo of his oracles against the nations presented in chapter 1, Amos warns of impending doom and encourages the people to repent and be saved from disaster.

Now hear this . . .

I gave you cleanness of teeth in all your cities, and lack of bread in all your places, yet you did not return to me, says the LORD. And I also withheld the rain from you when there were still three months to the harvest; I would send rain on one city, and send no rain on another city; one field would be rained upon, and the field on which it did not rain withered; so two or three towns wandered to one town to drink water, and were not satisfied; yet you did not return to me, says the LORD. I struck you with blight and mildew; I laid waste your gardens and your vineyards; the locust devoured your fig trees and your olive trees; yet you did not return to me, says the LORD. I sent among you a pestilence after the manner of Egypt; I killed your young men with the sword; I carried away your horses; and I made the stench of your camp go up into your nostrils; yet you did not return to me, says the LORD. I overthrew some of you, as when God overthrew Sodom and Gomorrah, and you were like a brand snatched from the fire; yet you did not return to me, says the LORD. (Amos 4:6-11)

Plague piled upon plague—famine, drought, blight, locusts, pestilence, sword, earthquake, and fire. A cascading shower of horror, like interconnected links in a chain, they follow and fall, repeatedly racing to an inevitable conclusion. This parade of plagues is reminiscent of the catalog of curses threatened to violators of the covenant. From the prophet's perspective, all of the disasters within nature and history are presented as a direct action of God. "I gave . . . I withheld . . . I struck . . . I sent . . . I overthrew." These occurrences experienced by Amos's audience are offered as object lessons in repentance, lessons that the people refused and failed to learn. After all of these confrontations, still the people did not change their ways. Religiosity is no substitute for repentance. They persisted in their transgressions, oblivious to guilt, free from remorse, and consistent in their unrepentance.

In the firestorm leveling the cities to rubble and ruin, a phrase pregnant with promise is heard; a spark of hope is seized: "You were like a brand snatched from the fire" (v. 11d). A hint of rescue and redemption is offered, signaling that out of the ashes of a civilization hitting bottom is a prospect for intervention.

The rectory at Epworth was engulfed in flames. Outside the burning house, Samuel and Susanna Wesley watched and prayed. Believing that his son was trapped inside, Samuel Wesley gave up the boy as lost and committed him to God's eternal care. With the help of neighbors, Susanna put legs on her prayers and rescued her six-year-old as "a brand from the burning." Seeing this child as special from not only a maternal but a divine perspective, Susanna nurtured and encouraged young John. Following completion of studies at Oxford, he entered the family business and was ordained an Anglican priest.

This "brand plucked from the burning" experienced another incinerating moment when he attended a prayer service at Aldersgate. "I felt my heart strangely warmed," John Wesley reported. "I felt I did trust Christ, Christ alone for salvation; and an assurance was given me that He had taken away my sins, even mine and saved me from the law of sin and death." From this "brand plucked from the burning" a flame of disciplined devotion and warm witness has continued in the Methodist tradition.

No Aldersgate revival of warm hearts and changed lives engulfed the recipients of Amos's witness. Following altar calls of famine and drought, blight and pestilence, war and devastation by earthquake and fire, a lament of divine disappointment is offered. "Yet you did not return to me" is the sad refrain voiced by the prophet on behalf of God. These convulsive calamities did not shake the people's complacency. The call to repentance was repeatedly given and consistently ignored. "Yet you did not return to me." What more could happen?

Now hear this . . . the prophetic proclamation continues, offering the final note in the score of God's dealings with the nation. As Israel in its formation had encountered God in Sinai, all of the nation should prepare to meet God. Merchants in the market, the soldiers of Samaria, the party crowd at the palace, the pilgrims at the shrines   all need to get ready. "Therefore thus I will do to you, O Israel; because I will do this to you, prepare to meet your God, O Israel!" (4:12).

Like a crudely lettered billboard on a mountain road in Appalachia, this announcement leaps into view. It is not a welcome sight, but a reminder of finitude and accountability. Such announcements offend the good taste and sophisticated sensitivity of successful, self-sufficient people. The impudence of persons living on the edge of "the good life" invading their self-absorption is not appreciated nor welcomed. Amos's announcement violates their understanding of their privileged position with the Almighty. The waiting for judgment will soon be over. "Prepare to confront your God!"

The prophet's pronouncement concludes in verse 13 with a hymn-like phrase:

> For lo, the one who forms the mountains, creates the wind, reveals
> his thoughts to mortals, makes the morning darkness, and treads on
> the heights of the earth—the LORD, the God of hosts, is his name!

This doxology offers a counterpoint to the plagues. The creator and sustainer of the universe reveals Himself to humankind. The shaper of the mountains, the animator of the winds, reveals Himself to humanity. From the valley depths to the mountain ridges of life, comes the God of hosts. The One who has given His name is offered as the last word and ultimate reality. The prophet speaks not for himself, nor for the religious or political establishment. Amos is a spokesperson for God—the God who formed the mountains, created the wind, revealed His intentions to humanity, transformed darkness into daybreak, and walks on the heights of the world—Yahweh, the God of Hosts.

Over the ship's public address system, the shrill pitch of the boatswain's whistle is heard. It is a signal for attention, which is followed by the announcement "Now hear this!" A message or announcement is about to be made. Listen up! You'd better hear this. In a time of crisis, all hands on deck hear the voice of the ship's commanding officer. "This is the captain speaking." With his identity and authority established, an order or directive will follow. "Man your battle stations . . . abandon ship . . . or . . . sweep down the deck fore and aft." Not attending to the announcement of what is being said could be disastrous and possibly life-threatening. Sailors ignoring announcements and refusing to follow orders are put on report. In the military, the consequences are clear for folks who tune out.

From the writings of Dietrich Bonhoeffer, who offered a heroic witness in Nazi Germany and died a martyr's death amid the stench and decay of a concentration camp, we hear these words on the importance of listening:

> The first service that one owes to others in fellowship consists of listening to them. He who can no longer listen to his brother will soon be no longer listening to God either; he will be doing nothing but prattle in the presence of God, too. This is the beginning of the death of the spiritual life, and in the end there is nothing left but spiritual chatter and clerical condescension arrayed in pious words. One who cannot listen long and patiently will presently be talking beside the point and never be speaking to others, albeit he be not conscious of it.[1]

Amidst the media plays for our attention, the clamor of the workplace, the uproar of the political arena, and the noise pollution that permeates all aspects of society, we need to take time to listen. There is a critical need to be still, to be quiet, and to listen. To listen, we center upon and tune in to the voice and the word of God. We quiet our anxiety. We stop talking. We refrain from bombarding God with our petitions and listen. We listen for a word that comes from before and beyond our time. We listen for a word and a reality that transcends the present.

Perhaps the most important thing we could do in worship is to "shut up." We could stop talking about the great things we are doing in the name of God. We should cease singing "how great we art" and experience anew an encounter with God. In worship we assemble to remember God's will and way and to recommit ourselves to divine expectations and righteous purposes. Such acts of genuine devotion will inform and direct our daily life and relationships. In worship we are able to discern and understand that life has meaning beyond money. Power and control, property and possessions are unworthy of ultimate concern. The abundance of life is not in things but in a loving, caring, supportive, and serving relationship with God and people.

In the tradition of the prophets, and fleshing out the Word of God in human form, came Jesus with an invitation to life and an offer of eternal hope. Often as he began to speak, he would say, "Let anyone with ears to hear listen!" (Mark 4:9). Are you listening? If so, who do you hear? What do you hear? And, what are you going to do about it?

Note

[1]Dietrich Bonhoeffer, *Life Together* (New York: Harper & Row, 1954, 1976) 97.

Chapter Five

You Did It to/for Me

Amos 5:1-17

Edd Rowell

Background

Brevard Childs suggested that "Historical-critical research has demonstrated . . . that the present form of the book of Amos has been reached only after a lengthy history of development which has shaped the material."[1] Such "shaping of the material" may be especially evident in Amos 5:1-17. Yet efforts to determine a "history of development" often result in preoccupation with supposed sources, presumed contexts, and alleged motives to the neglect of the text as it has come to us. It is "better to begin with the book [of Amos] in its completed form and to interpret first of all, and perhaps primarily, the completed text."[2] Indeed, "one should not assume . . . that editorial changes and additions are necessarily contaminants that must be excised to get back to the pure message of Amos."[3] We begin, then, with a translation of the Hebrew text.

Translation

[1]Hear this word I raise over you—
    a (funeral) dirge, O House of Israel.

[2]Virgin Israel has fallen
    and will not rise again;

she lies abandoned on her (own) ground
 (with) no one to raise her up.

[3]For thus says the Lord GOD:
 the city that sends out a battalion[4a]
  will be left with (only) a company[a]
 and the village that (fields) a company,
  with (only) a squad[a]
   for (defense of)[5b] the House of Israel.

[4]For (that reason),[6c] thus says the LORD to the House of Israel:
 Come to[7d] me and live.
[5]Do not consult[d] Bethel;
 do not turn to Gilgal;
  nor cross over to (the ancient sanctuary at) Beer-sheba.
 For Gilgal will surely be removed[8e]
  and Bethel shall become of no account.
[6]But turn to[d] the LORD and live,
 lest (the LORD) rush like a fire (upon) the House of Joseph
  and devour (it), with none in Bethel to quench (the fire).

[7]Those who make justice bitter,
 and abandon righteousness in the earth— . . .[9f]
[8](So unlike) the one
 who crafted (the constellations) Pleiades and Orion;
  (who) turns the deep darkness into morning
   and (then) darkens the day (to) night;
 (who) summons the waters of the sea
  and (then) pours them out onto the face of the earth
   —Yahweh (the LORD) is his name—[10g]
[9](who) bursts destruction upon the strong
  so that devastation comes upon (supposed) strongholds.

[10]. . . they hate those who call them to account
 and despise those who (insist on) dealing forthrightly.
[11]Therefore, because *you* have trampled the poor

and have extorted tribute payment of grain from (the poor),
you (may) have built luxurious houses—
     but you shall not (for long) dwell in them;
you (may) have planted delightful vineyards—
     but you shall not (for long) drink their wine.
12For I know your transgressions are many
     and your sins are numerous . . .
you who oppress honest folk,
     (who profit from) taking bribes,
               and who brush aside the needy who seek only fairness.
13Keeping quiet during such an evil time, (they say),
     is the smart thing to do.

14(But) seek^d (to do) good and not evil,
     that you may live;
and it may be that the LORD, the God of Hosts,
     will be with you—
               just as you have (always) said (it would be).
15Hate evil, love good,
     and establish just relations in all your dealings.
Thus it may be that the LORD, God of Hosts,
     will be gracious to those of Joseph who remain.

16Even so,^11h thus says Yahweh, the God of Hosts, the LORD:
     In all the marketplaces there will be wailing;
               in all the steeets they will cry out, "Alas! Woe!"
     Even farmers will be called on to mourn;
               professional mourners will be summoned to wail.
17Even in the vineyards there will be wailing
     for I will pass through the midst of you (in judgment),^12i
               says the LORD.

Commentary

The structure of the book of Amos may not be so simple as Amos scholars of an earlier generation supposed.[13] Yet neither is Amos as complex as, for example, Wolff and those who have followed in his train would have it.[14] The text seems to fall quite naturally into three parts: (1) prophetic pronouncements (oracles) against the nations, including Judah and Israel, 1:3–2:16; (2) sermons addressed to Israel, 3:1–5:17; and (3) (prophetic) visions of judgment, destruction, and discipline, 7:1–9:15; with an introduction (1:1-2) to the whole and a "book of woes" or warnings (5:18–6:14) as transition between the sermons and concluding visions.

Our text unit, then, is the last of the three "sermons" to Israel (3:1-15; 4:1-13; 5:1-17), each of which begins with the prophetic announcement "Hear this word."[15] (One also may note the three "sermons" are virtually the same length.) Rather than a haphazardly structured collection of oracles,[16] there appears to be a precise chiastic[17] order in Amos 5:1-17.[18]

> A 5:1-3, A lament for fallen Israel
> 　　B 5:4-6, Turn to the LORD and live
> 　　　　C 5:7-13, A litany of condemnation
> 　　B' 5:14-15, Turn to righteousness and live
> A' 5:16-17, A lament for fallen Israel[19]

A lament for fallen Israel, 5:1-3. Verse 1 introduces the "sermon" with the prophet's call to "Hear this word" (see 3:1; 4:1; cf. 8:4). That the prophet is in fact being a prophet and speaking a "word of the LORD" is stated at 3:1. "Of the LORD" is lacking at 4:1 and here, but should be understood.

Walther Eichrodt defines the "prophetic word of God" as "the particular proclamation of the divine will for particular situations."[20] This lamentation or funeral dirge, then, was God's word to Israel at this particular time. It was a time when the judgment and/or discipline of the LORD was about to fall upon Israel. It was a situation Israel had brought upon Israel's own self by adulteration of the justice and righteousness required by covenant with the LORD. The result of Israel's sin was so certain that Amos already could sing the death song over Israel. Israel was as good as dead but did not know it. Wake up! Amos cries, "hear this word" before it is too late.

The "dirge" or "lament" was an established practice, with an established poetic meter (qinah, "dirge," designates both the "death song"

and the meter in which it was set). Eventually, funeral dirges were prepared and performed by "professionals" (see v. 16). Probably the earliest
recorded example of such a dirge is David's song over Saul and
Jonathan (2 Sam 1:17-27; see also 2 Sam 3:33-34, over Abner). Amos's
funeral song is very brief—only the four or two lines of verse 2. Verse
3 recasts the dirge with more specific imagery.

It is tempting to wax hermeneutic over the designation "Virgin
Israel" (v. 2; cf. esp. Jer 18:13; 31:4, 21). It seems best however to read
its simplest meaning: Israel will be cut down before fulfilling Israel's
destiny (a virgin is "childless"), a graphic picture of Israel's tragic,
untimely demise. Of course, "Virgin Israel" may be biting sarcasm:
Israel's destruction is self-inflicted, the result of Israel's unfaithfulness to
the covenant and to Israel's covenant partner. Israel has turned covenant
righteousness and justice wrongside out and upside down. "Virgin"
Israel? No! Israel is rather a blatant adulterer.

Notice the progressive parallelism of verse 2: Israel is fallen / Israel
will not rise / Israel is forsaken / No one will raise Israel. Israel has forsaken those of her own household (the poor and needy within its gates,
vv. 11-12); Israel will be forsaken even in its own household, on its own
ground. Sin too—like the proverbial chickens—always comes home
to roost.

In verse 2 the description of Israel's demise is graphic but in general
terms. In verse 3 the description is startling in its stark detail: each community will send out its armies, and in every instance only one in ten
will return. (From earliest times, Israel maintained a standing army
composed of "thousands, hundreds, fifties, tens" from the various tribes
and then the city-states: see Exod 18:21, 25; 2 Sam 18:1-4; and esp.
Num 31:14.) The imagery is graphic but probably at the time would
suggest allusions that now are lost to us. But the meaning is plain: Israel
will be decimated, virtually eliminated as a viable people.

This lament over fallen Israel (1–3) is chiastically mirrored in verses
16-17 where the imagery is more specifically funereal: Israel's destruction is an accomplished fact. Mourning over Israel is as universal as
Israel's destruction—in the marketplace and streets, in the fields and
vineyards. Everyone is affected. The immediate cause of Israel's whole-
sale destruction (vv. 1-3) and the resulting universal mourning (vv.

16-17) is stated in the final phrase of verse 17: "for I will pass through the midst of you, says the LORD." This seems obviously an allusion to the original "passover" (Exod 11:4-6; 12:12). The LORD will pass through Israel as He passed through Egypt, destruction in His wake. (This theme of the terrible judgment of the Lord's appearing is taken up in vv. 18ff. as "the day of the LORD.")

Turn to the Lord and live, 5:4-6. Amos's lament finds relief in this "invitation" to repentance. The verb rendered above as "come to," "consult," and "turn to" is routinely translated "seek" (KJV, RSV, NRSV, etc.). In the Old Testament, persons *seek* God or something related (Torah, sanctuary, justice, peace, wisdom, etc.). Such seeking always includes active involvement, as stated in one English equivalent: "to be *occupied* with" (TDOT 3:289). The classic invitation of Isaiah 55:6ff. suggests such seeking involves turning to the LORD and away from evil, that is, repentance. (In the New Testament, this seeking is for the "kingdom," that is, God's rule, "and his righteousness," Matt 6:33.)

Bethel, Gilgal, and Beer-sheba (v. 6) were ancient shrines and long-established worship centers. In Amos's day they were popular pilgrimage centers. (Today we may compare the "Holy Land" and other historic places, or even one's ancestral "home church" or childhood baptism site.) Do *not* seek Bethel or Gilgal or Beer-sheba (v. 5) suggests an idolatry of place: the Israelites had substituted attendance at the sanctuary and the related rituals for the worship of God and for righteousness or right relationships. Attendance at an ancient shrine and participation in the established ritual is not just insufficient; without real worship and genuine repentance, it is idolatrous. Only an active seeking of the LORD—with the repentance such seeking involves—is sufficient.

The chiastic parallel (vv. 14-15) makes this plain. The invitation is to turn to the *good* and away from the *evil,* to "establish justice" or, better, just relations. Seeking the LORD involves not just right worship but right living, right relationships. In the event of such genuine repentance, we may hope for grace, for the LORD's forgiveness (v. 15). (Whether this grace is for what is left of Israel after the anticipated destruction or whether those who repent and thus are spared will constitute "the remnant" is not clear.)

A litany of condemnation, 5:7-13. Were Amos 5:1-17 a play, this text unit would be the climax. For this prophetic oracle or "sermon," verses 7-13 form the chiastic center, the focal point on which all else turns. These verses constitute a litany of condemnation against Israel, a recitation of Israel's "many" and "great" sins (v. 12) that are summed up as "turning justice to bitterness" and "trampling righteousness/right relations into the ground" (v. 7). The sins for which Israel is condemned are not against the LORD but against Israel's own people. This foreshadows the pronouncement of the Great Judgment parable: "Just as you did/did not do it to one of the least of these, you did/did not do it to me" (Matt 25:40, 45).

Some interpreters see verses 8-9 as a later editorial "doxology" (cf. 4:13; 9:5-6) that is out of place and should precede verse 7 so as not to interrupt the continuity of verses 7 and 10ff. (as in NAB, REB, etc.). In their present position, verses 8-9 indicate an interjection following the summary indictment of verse 7: Amos interjects an aside to the effect that Israel's sin is so unlike Israel's covenant God. The doxology contrasts Israel with Israel's God. Those with means in Israel, the rich and powerful, have trampled the poor and powerless. In stark contrast, "the one who made" all creation (v. 8), whose means are limitless, uses position and power only in judgment against those who have abused position and power (v. 9).

The litany of condemnation against Israel in verses 7-12 is rather straightforward. The rich and powerful are condemned for their abuses of power—their mistreatment of the powerless for personal gain (vv. 11-12)—and also for their abuse of those who would call them to account (v. 10). They have turned justice wrongside out and righteousness upside down. The basic message of Amos is that in a time of seeming prosperity, the pervasive and unrestrained religious and social corruption in Israel has sealed Israel's doom. Indeed, prosperity if undisciplined often breeds pride, abuse of privilege, condescension toward those less fortunate, and even ingratitude, as Hosea so clearly recognized: "When they were fed full, they forgot the LORD" (Hos 13:6).

Verses 7-12 require little explanation, but verse 13 is difficult. Various interpretations are possible, for example, "keeping quiet in such evil times is the smart thing to do" (TEV). That is, "so evil is the time" (Moffatt) that the prudent person will not speak up (either for oneself or for another) for fear of bringing trouble on oneself. Otherwise, Amos may be saying simply that to speak up is a waste of time: the times are so bad that no amount of talking will do any good. Of course, if this is what Amos meant, he said it tongue-in-cheek or sarcastically because Amos himself was certainly not keeping silent. At any rate, "such [an] evil time" apparently refers to the fact that even those charged with overseeing justice, the "courts," are themselves terminally corrupt (cf. v. 10).

In verse 10 the usual translation "in the gate" refers to the community gathering place, the "town meeting" place where community matters were discussed and settled under the oversight of elders or other community leaders, including prophets, that is, who "reprove" or "speak the truth." To speak up, verse 13 suggests, was not only a waste of time but possibly even dangerous. Amos nevertheless was speaking up, so the advice of verse 13 may well be sarcastic criticism of those leaders who should have been speaking out (reproving, v. 10) against the rampant religious and social corruption in Israel. Verse 13 may well be a climactic word in Amos's sermon. Others may think they are doing the smart thing to keep quiet. Amos himself could not be silent.

Application for Preaching and Teaching

You Did It to/for Me
Amos 5:1-17; Matthew 25:31-46

During a Monday's lunchtime I heard a rather arresting report on C-SPAN's "Washington Journal" on National Public Radio. I took no notes, but I recall that the journalist said the gap between the haves and have-nots in the USA has now become greater than in any other industrialized nation in the world. The figures were something like this: the richest four percent control ninety-six percent of the wealth, while the other ninety-six percent control only four percent of the wealth of the nation.

Such figures are startling, especially for a nation that prides itself on a supposed "level playing field." In fact the field is not level, and seems to become less so every day. In spite of national propaganda to the contrary, the USA has become just another society where the rich keep getting richer and the poor keep getting poorer.

Of course, it is an old tune, one we have heard many times before. Even Jesus said we will always have the poor with us (Mark 14:7 and par.). And there are indeed substantial psychological, sociological, and political reasons why the poor tend to get poorer and the rich tend to get richer. However, the misappropriation of Jesus' poor-always-with-us saying and all the psychological, sociological, and political research we can muster cannot hide the fact that much of the disparity between the haves and have-nots is due simply to greed, injustice, and the blatant abuse of position and power at the expense of the positionless and powerless. How often is even the most average among us guilty of catering to the rich (who might repay us) while ignoring the poor (who cannot repay us)? This is not just a rich/poor situation. All of us are involved.

The situation was much the same in Jesus' time, and, even earlier, in Amos's day. In fact, the prophetic message we call Amos is *the* classic text regarding such a situation. The theme of Amos is best stated in 5:21-24, and particularly in the majestic cadences of the King James Version: "I hate, I despise your feast days. . . . But let justice [orig. judgment] roll down like waters, and righteousness like a mighty stream." True piety, genuine worship, Amos said, is not to be found in the sanctuary or in the ritual but in social justice, in right relationships. But the best description of the situation is probably 5:1-18, especially verses 7-13.

Amos prophesied during the long reign of Jeroboam II (786–746 B.C.), probably right in the middle of the eighth century B.C. The time has been described as

> a time of great prosperity, notable religious piety, and apparent security. But Amos saw that prosperity was limited to the wealthy, and that it fed on injustice and on oppression of the poor. Religious observance was insincere, and security more apparent than real. With compassion and courage [Amos] preached that God would punish the nation. (TEV introduction to Amos)

The whole of Amos and especially 5:7-13 is an almost unrelenting condemnation of those responsible for the religious and social corruption that pervaded the nation of Israel. It was this universal impiety and social dysfunction that had brought on a situation in which the rich kept getting richer and the poor, poorer.

In general, let us agree that the disparity between rich and poor may be as great now as in Amos's day. We may even concede the possibility that abuse of power by the few rich is often at the expense of the many poor. The problem is, there are neither many rich among us to take responsibility or poor among us to be victims. We are rather encamped on that vast middle ground we call the middle class. So, what does Amos's message have to do with the most of us?

Even those of us in the middle contribute to the rich/poor disparity by our catering to the rich to the neglect of the poor. Even if such action is unconscious or unintended, it is just as real. The reason is apparent: the rich may contribute to our success or at least to our survival; the poor not only may not but cannot. Are you and I guilty of "trampling the poor" or "pushing aside the needy" (5:11, 12) in our anxiety to get our share of success or at least of survival? Are we guilty of ignoring any word or scorning any messenger that suggests we may be part of the problem (5:10)? Pray God we are not guilty. Yet we well may be.

More appropriate to us, I think, is Amos 5:13, which apparently is a piece of biting sarcasm from Amos. This verse is difficult to interpret but may be paraphrased as follows: "During such an evil time, the smart thing to do (some say) is to keep quiet." Amos himself did not keep quiet. He spoke out loudly and plainly and with sustained condemnation of the religious and social corruption he saw all around. Amos 5:13 suggests Amos saved a special kind of scorn for those who should be speaking out but were silent for fear of bringing trouble on themselves. These so-called prudent folk not only did not speak up; they did nothing else either.

Amos's catalog of offenses in 5:7-13 focuses on the inhumanity of humanity. The theme passage in 5:21-24 suggests that worship is genuine only if it includes or results in right relations with others. Doing the right thing by our fellow humans is better than any ritual or liturgy.

In fact, without such right relationships, worship is meaningless, empty, vain.

Amos's prophetic word is plain. Even so, Jesus picks up on that word in his story of the Great Judgment (Matt 25:31-46) and makes it plainer. On that day, Jesus said, some will be blessed and some will be condemned, and neither will really understand why. The cursed will be condemned for what they did *not* do, the blessed for what they *did* do. William Barclay, with his inimitable ability to make the message plain, suggests three things about such actions.[21]

First, these are ordinary, everyday things: a meal for one who is hungry, a drink for one who is thirsty, welcome for a stranger, comfort for one sick, visiting the prisoner—all of them things anyone can do. We may not have our thousands to give, but any one of us can do this kind of caring, helping, supporting, comforting, forgiving thing. Such things Amos apparently saw little or none of in eighth-century-B.C. Israel. How much of such things do we see today? They are the kind of simple, ordinary, everyday, but essential actions of kindness and caring that we do for each other when justice rolls down and righteousness flows.

Second, these simple things get done as a matter of course, as the natural outgrowth of a right relationship with God. That is, they are quite uncalculating. There is no conscious expectation of reward or recompense. In Jesus' story, those who were blessed for their deeds acted naturally, their actions springing from a loving heart. Those who were condemned for not doing the right thing confirm this: they would have acted, they said, if they had known it would be to their benefit.

Finally, the grand truth of Jesus' story and of Amos's prophesy is that doing the right thing for the sake of others is in the final analysis done to and for God. "You did it," Jesus says, "to/for me." So, God said through Amos (5:6, 14), "Seek me and live. . . . [that is] Seek good and not evil, that you may live."

> I looked for God but God I could not see.
> I searched for Christ but Christ eluded me.
> I sought my brother/sister and found all three.

Notes

[1]Brevard S. Childs, *Introduction to the Old Testament as Scripture* (Philadelphia: Fortress Press, 1979) 399.

[2]Roy F. Melugin, "Amos" in *Harper's Bible Commentary* (HBC), ed. James L. Mays et al. (San Francisco: Harper & Row, 1988) 720a.

[3]John C. Shelley, "Amos" in the *Mercer Commentary on the Bible* (MCB), ed. Watson E. Mills et al. (Macon GA: Mercer University Press, 1994) 744a.

[4a]The allusion is to military casualties, hence the reference to military units. The O.T. terms "thousands," "hundreds," and "tens," however, require some explanation. The more contemporary terms "battalion," "company," and "squad" seem appropriate.

[5b]As "Virgin Israel" is fallen and abandoned with none to come to its aid, the nation will be defenseless in the coming judgment.

[6c]The conj. ("for," "since," "because"; German has *darum* here) may be better expressed as simply "*Yet*, thus says. . . . "

[7d]"Come to" (v. 4), "consult" (v. 5), and "turn to" (v. 6) may be simply "seek" (v. 14), the usual translation (e.g., NRSV, NAB, NJB, NIV). Something more seems to be required here. In the OT, use of *darash* ("seek") is predominantly theological and requires either a theological rendering or at least an awareness of a more-than-literal content. It may well be that " 'Seek me and live' in 5:4-6 is equivalent to a summons to repentance" (TDOT 3:301). Indeed, "seek me" may be misleading "since what is meant is something like 'make your way to me' (REB) or 'turn to me' " (MCB 749b).

[8e]That is, exiled.

[9f]Some text critics suppose vv. 8-9 should come before v. 7 so as not to disrupt the apparent continuity of vv. 7 and 10-12 (as, e.g., in NAB and REB; Moffatt appends 5:8-9 to 4:13).

[10g]Some text critics would also relocate this line, either before v. 8 or after v. 9 (as in NAB). As an interjection into this paragraph, however, it seems rightly placed.

[11h]The compound adverb "therefore" of course follows upon vv. 7-12; but here "even so" makes logical the transition from the call to repentance that intervenes (vv. 13-15).

[12i]The figurative language may have to do with (broken) covenant or may be a reference to the "passing through" Egypt preceding the Exodus. Some addition such as "in judgment" seems to be indicated even though the specific allusion is uncertain.

[13]George Adam Smith saw three groups of oracles under the one title "Words of Amos": (1) chaps. 1–2; (2) chaps. 3–6; and (3) chaps. 7–9 (*The Book of the Twelve Prophets*, 2 vols, The Expositor's Bible [New York: Hodder & Stoughton and Doran, 1896, 1898; 2nd ed., New York: Harper, 1928] 1:61-64). William Rainey Harper also saw Amos as falling *primarily* into three main parts: (1) Oracles, chaps. 1–2; (2) Sermons, chaps. 3–6; and (3) Visions, chaps. 7–9. Indeed, Harper curmudgeonly remarked: "It is unfortunate that some recent critics seem as blind to the simplicity of Amos's style of expression as were the older critics to its refined nature." (*A Critical and Exegetical Commentary on Amos and Hosea*, International Critical Commentary [Edinburgh: T. & T. Clark; New York: Scribner's, 1905] outline on cxxxii; quote on cxxxviii.)

[14]As John Bright pointedly remarked, in a review of Wolff's very influential commentary on Joel and Amos. Bright thought it rather incredible that redaction critics could posit as many as eight levels of "editorial activity" for the short text of Amos (*Interpretation* 25 [1971]: 355-56).

[15]Michael L. Barré aptly characterizes these "sermons" as "summonses to hear Yahweh's word," in "Amos," *The New Jerome Biblical Commentary* (NJBC), ed. Raymond E. Brown et al. (Englewood Cliffs NJ: Prentice Hall, 1990) 210.

[16]As suggested, e.g., by Charles F. Kraft, "The Book of Amos," *The Interpreter's One-Volume Commentary on the Bible* (IOVC), ed. Charles M. Laymon (Nashville/New York: Abingdon Press, 1971) 469a.

[17]See "Chiasm" in the *Mercer Dictionary of the Bible,* ed. Watson E. Mills et al. (Macon GA: Mercer University Press, 1990) 141-42.

[18]See, e.g., Shelley, "Amos," MCB 749b; see also recent studies cited there.

[19]Cf. and contrast the chiastic outlines in MCB (749b) and in NJBC (210b). If this chiastic structure appears a bit too precise for the primitive competence of an eighth-century-B.C. "cowboy," let me commend David Hall's excellent apology against "The Argument from Primitive Culture" in *The Seven Pillories of Wisdom* (Macon: Mercer University Press, 1990).

[20]*Theology of the Old Testament*, vol. 2, trans. J. A. Baker (Philadelphia: Westminster, 1967) 72.

[21]See William Barclay, *The Gospel of Matthew*, vol. 2 (chaps. 11-28), 2d ed., The Daily Study Bible (Philadelphia: Westminster Press, 1958) 358-61.

Chapter Six

Feast or Famine?

Amos 5:18-27

David J. Reimer

Background

The "Day of the Lord" passage in Amos is one of the most memorable in the book, and has been one of the most influential outside it. Although sounded briefly, and only here, Amos's prophecy of a coming day when Yahweh would turn against God's people has occasioned much debate. Many agree that Amos's oracle preserves for us the first instance of this theme; but it occurs occasionally elsewhere, continuing into the New Testament where it is found in the first preserved letter of Paul (1 Thess 5:2). Our passage also contains one of the most evocative calls to justice in the Hebrew Bible (5:24).

The theme of the Day is confined to three verses (5:18-20), but the interpretation of this "Day" raises questions about the relationship of these verses to their context, as well as about their connections to other "Day of the Lord" passages outside Amos. This passage is further complicated by striking variations in literary style, as well as obscure references in 5:25-27. Fortunately, the Hebrew text has few difficulties in this section, and whatever limited textual comments are needed will be offered as problems arise.

Since so many questions about the interpretation of the Day turn on how one relates the components of the passage, we will first examine each section in turn before looking at them together.

Micro Structure

Our passage divides neatly into three short sections: 5:18-20, the Day of Yahweh; 5:21-24, cult rejected/justice demanded; 5:25-27, futility of sacrifice. Each of these units has its own marks of coherence and, likewise, features that set each apart. In the first unit we hear the voice of the prophet addressing the people. The second unit contains speech from Yahweh in carefully measured poetic lines. Yahweh's voice continues in the third unit, but now prose takes over from poetry.

The Day of Yahweh—5:18-20. A sharp outcry begins the first section, marking it off from the preceding oracle, and is pronounced against those who "desire" the Day of Yahweh. This stark introduction leads into the content of the expectation and, more to the point, its reversal. The repetition of the description that the Day will be darkness and not light bounds the brief announcement (vv. 18b, 20a). Both the opening and closing verses are obviously poetic, forming a neat envelope around the message in the middle.

The central verse 19 contains a word picture of the Day in more expansive and prosaic terms than verses 18 and 20. Two scenarios are sketched: in the first, a man flees a lion, only to meet a bear; in the second, someone arrives home, only to be bitten by a snake. Commentators are divided as to whether this is a single "story"[1] or whether the two panels should be seen as distinct.[2] In the first case, the vignettes build to a climax; in the second, they are mutually reinforcing. There is little by way of evidence to decide the matter. It is worth noting that (a) although prosaic, these lines contain more than a touch of poetic balance, and the structure of Hebrew poetry lends itself to a heightening or intensifying movement; and (b) the subject in verse 19a ("someone") is unrepeated in verse 19b, suggesting a carry-over of actor from the first half to the second.

Neither of these arguments is conclusive, but it is appealing to read the verse as a single "story." A man in the country encounters a lion, but escaping that predicament he runs into a bear. He makes it safely home and leans back in relief—only to be bitten by a snake! The implication is that the bite is lethal. This is a perfect nightmare. The escalation in verse 19a is already apparent. "Lion" occurs in the Old Testament eighty times; "bear" is much more rare, occurring only twelve times. What are the chances of escaping one to be chased by the other? The gap between apparent security and real danger is even greater in verse 19b, with the safety of home harboring the serpent's poison.

Those who "desire" (v. 18) the Day of Yahweh can expect this kind of gap between security and danger. The word used for "desiring" is a strong one. It is used in a variety of contexts, but usually has to do with bodily appetites or cravings (Num 11:4; 1 Chron 11:17) or with one's personal wishes (1 Kgs 11:37), and as such can also be used with sexual connotations (Ps 45:11). On occasion, the term also has some spiritual overtones, as in Isaiah 26:9. The use in 5:18 is echoed in Jeremiah 17:16, in one of Jeremiah's laments at the message he must proclaim.

Little or no information is given here concerning the specifics of the coming day of doom. On the other hand, this tightly framed unit gives us a clear picture of the emotive side of the Day of Yahweh: it is eagerly desired and anticipated; it will be disastrous in the most terrifying fashion.

Cult rejected/justice demanded—5:21-24. A change of voice signals the start of a new unit. No longer is the voice the prophet's; rather, it is the Lord's. Here, the poetry is even more regular than in the preceding verses, but without the "envelope" structure that gives verses 18-20 such a defined shape. The Hebrew of verse 22 presents some difficulties. The context is that of first-person singular verbs ("I . . . "), but verse 22a has a second-person plural ("You [pl.] . . . "). Not only that, but the opening words, "even though" hang without any corresponding conclusion. The clause appears to be stranded.

Commentators generally see a problem here,[3] and older commentators were not averse to conjuring up some missing bit! The Old Greek translation (LXX) slightly shifted the sense of the opening words to yield a sense much like that given in the RSV or NIV: "*Even though* you bring me . . ."[4] While possible, this is not the most natural translation. Andersen and Freedman offer a translation that nicely captures the awkwardness of the Hebrew, while making some sense of the text as it stands:

> Whatever you sacrifice to me
> —your burnt offerings and gifts—
> I cannot accept
> —your peace offerings and fat cattle—
> I cannot approve.[5]

It remains difficult to accommodate verse 22a into the structure of this unit. The rest, however, follows regular poetic lines that, in a relentless series of first person verbs, pronounce Yahweh's rejection of the people's cultic observance. It begins with a double announcement ("I hate, I despise . . .") that sets the tone for what follows. Yahweh will not "enjoy," "accept," "look at," or "listen to" their religious behavior.[6] This chain is broken only by the command in verse 23a for the "noise of your songs" to be removed.

Verse 23 forms the pithy conclusion, with the insistence (echoing v. 23a) that justice and righteousness "roll down" like abundant waters. This image, as striking as it is, is difficult to account for in context. Paul[7] suggests that it may be drawn from Canaanite mythology, a probable enough source.[8]

Futility of sacrifice—5:25-27. The theme of the third unit continues that of the second. Here poetry is abandoned, and the speech—still the voice of Yahweh—is straight prose. Andersen and Freedman observe that "[v]erse 25 is the longest individual clause in Amos,"[9] its ponderous phrasing standing in stark contrast to the sharp poetry of verses 21-24.

Each verse here forms a separate component of another indictment of Israel's worship and the punishment that awaits. Verse 25 recalls worship in the wilderness; verse 26 turns to the images Israel has made for itself; verse 27 announces the verdict—exile, "beyond Damascus." The combination of these elements forms a self-contained oracle focusing again on religious failings. Often Amos's prophecies are characterized as dealing with social injustice, but this assumption can be overstated.

Here the emphasis is on cultic behavior and its repugnance (vv. 21-24) and futility (vv. 25-27). It may be, of course, that lack of "justice and righteousness" impaired worship, but this remains an implication in this passage, at least. The rhetorical question of verse 25 points out that Yahweh's protection of the people, at a time when their situation was at its most precarious, came *not* through their religious observance, but rather, it is implied, through Yahweh's gracious care. In spite of this, they have made gods that cannot protect them. These false gods will be borne into exile, as the people themselves will be exiled "beyond Damascus" by their true God (v. 27).

The names "Sakkuth" and "Kaiwan" (v. 26) are not familiar to most readers and, as oddities, have naturally attracted the attention of commentators. Paul's illuminating discussion convincingly relates these deities to Assyrian astral worship, and especially the practice of carrying divine images in festal processions.[10] The final phrase, "says the LORD, whose name is the God of hosts," recalls the three "doxologies" of Amos, each of which has "the LORD is his name," the first of them including "God of hosts" (4:13; 5:8; 9:6).

Biblical scholars have often suggested that these verses are "secondary" in the book, not deriving from the prophet himself. The strongest argument in favor of this view is the heavily prosaic nature of the language. Amos's oracles are so consistently poetic that this prose passage understandably stands out. On the other hand, nothing in this passage requires that it be dated later than Amos, and the reference to Assyrian astral worship is well-suited to his own period. Still, the language is nicely ambiguous. Assyrian religion is thought to have been a growing problem in Judah under Manasseh (cf. 2 Kgs 21:1-9, esp. vv. 3, 5), and exile "beyond Damascus" would be as fitting under the later Babylonians as it was under the Assyrians.

Macro Structure

With such well-formed units, one can easily see why they are so often taken in isolation one from the other. Further, while verses 21-24 and 25-27 appear to have some thematic connection in their harsh attitude towards the cult, verses 18-20 have little in common with them and seem to be linked only by juxtaposition.

There is an explicit verbal link between the second and third units, in the word "gift/offering," *mincha*, which appears both in verse 22a and verse 25a. But their relationship is much stronger than simply this shared item of vocabulary. Verses 21-25 outline a radical rejection of the cult by Yahweh, so radical that it borders on the unthinkable. Surely it is impossible that a deity should reject out of hand the devotion of worshipers? Would not rejection on this scale undermine not only religious but also social and political identity?

The very fabric of Israelite society is at stake here. If feasts are pointless, if the nation's guilt cannot be atoned, if God refuses to be placated or involved with Israel, what is left? How can there be "justice and righteousness" (v. 24) when the ground of justice—the religious life of the people—is gone? Surely Amos goes too far here, and his message becomes nonsensical.

This is the point at which verses 25-27 make their contribution to the "logic" of the passage. Amos seems to think that the cult is expendable and unnecessary for a "just society." Rather than this being unthinkable, however, verses 25-27 point towards the experience of the wilderness. Exodus traditions do not play a large part in Amos's prophecies, only appearing here, at 2:10 and, in a rather surprising context, at 9:7. In those passages, the emphasis is on God's ability to act on behalf of God's people. Here, the focus is on the people's actions in the rhetorical question: "Did you bring to me sacrifices and offerings the forty years in the wilderness . . . ?" The answer is: No, they did not! Yet, the implication is, this was the time of greatest bonding and affection between Yahweh and Israel.

Such is the nearly contemporary picture in Hosea 2, where the wilderness was a time of alluring and devotion (Hos 2:14-15) and provided a vision for future fidelity (Hos 2:16-23; cf. Jer 2:2). But this time of devotion knew none of the sacrificial/festive trappings that Amos is rejecting. Given the precedent of the wilderness, Amos's unthinkable rejection is drawn into the realm of the possible. Further, verse 26 continues, the "devotion" offered in these cultic acts is not shown towards Yahweh in any case, but to gods identified with the Assyrians. Right, says the prophet, off you go, taking your false gods with you.

Is there anything here that connects the Day of Yahweh oracle of verses 18-20? Apparently not—or if there is, it is not so easily seen as the cultic connections in the latter part of our passage. But to get some sense of the possibilities, we must move beyond the bounds of 5:18-27 itself and notice something about the larger context.

Other Thematic Links

The very first word of the Day of the Lord oracle suggests connections within the context. "Woe!" or "alas" (Hebrew *hoy*) has attracted a great deal of attention for such a little word, and not only among commentators. A number of specialized studies have been devoted to "woe" oracles, with a great deal of disagreement to be found in them. One thing that is widely agreed—while its significance is still debated—is the use of this term in lament or funerary contexts (cf. 1 Kgs 13:30; Jer 22:18). A variant form of this term is used in Amos 5:16 where the context is explicitly mourning ("in all the streets they shall say, 'Alas! alas!' " = *ho ho*). While this connection has been observed,[11] it has not been pursued. Yet, it points to a valuable trajectory in coming to terms with the—rather unspecific—announcement of the gloomy Day of Yahweh.

In 5:16-17, wailing moves from town streets into the fields, and farmers are called to mourn. This echoes the settings in 5:10-13, where town and field are again in the foreground. The mourning motif runs like a scarlet thread throughout the chapter, as 5:1 announces a word taken up "in lamentation," almost as a superscription for the chapter as a whole. If we look in the other direction, 6:1 continues this theme, with yet another announcement of woe, implicating a further series of those who will have cause to mourn.

Such thematic links suggest that, while chapter 5 may have an apparently disjointed feel, closer examination shows these juxtapositions to carry more significance than we might at first have thought. Into this web of connections, joining mourning, agricultural settings, and feasting and cultic interests, we have the brief announcement of the Day of Yahweh. It means death and darkness rather than life and light, as seems to be the expectation of the hearers. (Note the striking resonances in Job's renunciation of life and light and his wish for death and darkness in Job 3:1-10.)

A final reference in Amos prepares us to cast the net more widely, beyond the bounds of this book alone. Amos 8:9-10 also draws these elements tightly together, but seldom is this passage connected to 5:18-27 or to the Day of the Lord imagery. Mays is willing to make some link, but this is piece-meal, relating the darkness of 8:9 to 5:18, the cultic imagery of 8:10 to 5:21, and the mourning to 5:16.[12] Others connect the darkness imagery as well,[13] but go no further than this. Commentators are generally more interested in the possibility of an eclipse providing a context for 8:9-10. Furthermore, understandings of "the Day" usually preclude taking 8:9-10 in these terms; and while the "day" in the opening phrase "in that day" is formulaic, "day" is repeated twice more, at the close of both verses.

The network of resonances noticed by Mays suggests that these passages be taken together. If we do so, we see even more clearly that an expected day of light, life, and festivity will instead be a day of death, darkness, and destruction. Both in 5:10-27 and in 8:9-10, cultic observances are implicated in the prophet's denunciations.

Proclaiming the Day of the Lord

Before suggesting how this powerful word might be proclaimed today, let us draw the threads of these observations together. Amos 5:18-27 seemed to be made up of compatible but loosely connected poetic units. Closer attention to context suggested that this juxtaposition was not merely accidental, but built up into a coherent picture, in which expectation for joyous feasting would be met instead by disaster and punishment. Key features in this picture were supernatural darkness, rejection of cultic service, reversal of agricultural fortunes, and lament and mourning. Probing beyond the bounds of the passage, echoes of similar motifs connected with a "day" were found in Amos (8:9-10). Further confirmation could be found in Amos's near contemporary Hosea 9:1-9 (see especially 9:5), and in another major repository of "Day of the Lord" imagery, Joel (1:13-15; 2:1-2; 3:13-15), all of which share the same web of connections as Amos 5.

Our task is not to develop the full academic apparatus of argument and evidence needed to clarify all of the Day of the Lord traditions in the Bible; that would require a book. But we have done sufficient research to suggest how Amos's Day of the Lord functions, which runs counter to much that one finds in commentaries and Old Testament theologies.[14] The massive influence of Gerhard von Rad is widely felt on this question. His 1959 article[15] convinced many, and precluded further thought about Amos 5:18-20, for a reason that is immediately apparent.

Von Rad believed that since the Amos passage—foundational though it was—provided no clues in itself as to the nature of the Day, it would have to be set aside and the fuller picture gleaned elsewhere. As he turned to other traditions, the military imagery seemed to dominate, and so von Rad associated Yahweh's Day with traditions of holy war— a subject on which he was writing a small monograph at the time. When he returned to the Amos passage, the theme of darkness, so pronounced there, was naturally associated with this martial imagery of holy war.

There are significant problems with von Rad's analysis, not least of which is the trouble with "holy war" itself. It has been widely argued since von Rad that "holy war" is a late, idealistic construct, developing well beyond the time of Amos. If this is the case, as I believe it to be, then Amos's Day of the Lord cannot originate in this later ideology. Further, von Rad was wrong to abandon the crucial Amos passage so quickly. Perhaps something of scholarly fashion is at work here.

For von Rad and his contemporaries, the biblical text was often seen much more readily in its parts than as a whole. The tendency of form criticism—an approach with which von Rad was deeply allied— is to relate remote passages together in the effort to find a generic pattern. This is exactly von Rad's method here. However, context has become an ever more important arbiter of meaning in more recent times as the biblical text in its final form has been prized once more, and scholars are less willing to put asunder what has long been joined together.

Others have developed von Rad's idea in different directions. One commonly reads in commentaries of the Day of the Lord being the notion widely held in ancient Israel that Yahweh would march at the head of God's armies, vanquish Israel's foes, and bring them peace and prosperity, or light and life, in Amos's terms. Such a scenario attempts to be faithful to the context of Amos while incorporating the military origins identified by von Rad.[16] Some commentators further identify the Day with the tradition that "a true sovereign could win his wars in a single day." Others attempt to link the war motifs with the festival setting.[17] While this might be appropriate in later literature when the motif has been developed, it nonetheless does violence to the Amos context where, as von Rad fully realized, martial imagery is simply absent.

Mowinckel's notion that the Day of Yahweh was rooted in the cult has had only a minority following. Partly this is due to the great success of von Rad's interpretation; partly it was held back by the excesses of Mowinckel's own theories that attempted to reconstruct in detail aspects of the cult—the enthronement of Yahweh, or theophany for example—that many found unconvincing. Our close reading of the Amos text, however, combined with attention to parallels found elsewhere, suggest that Mowinckel was not far off the mark.

Amos 5 is a lament, and as the lament develops—with the occasional detour in verse 6-9 and 14-15—one sees a picture of a people punished. They are decimated (v. 3) because of the injustices perpetrated in society (vv. 10-13). At that point we pick up the hints of expectations of prosperity: it is greed that has motivated oppression, the desire to live in posh homes, have the best fields, the best stocked larders and wine cellars. But exactly this sort of greed—which would culminate in the harvest celebrations in the autumn festival—provokes an angry God to wrath.

Instead of contented feasting in the vineyards and fields, there will be wailing and lamentation (vv. 16-17). Expectations for plenty at Yahweh's festival are dashed, for it becomes a day of darkness, and not light (vv. 18-20). Yahweh will turn away from any aspect of the festival: its assemblies, sacrifices, offerings, songs, and dances (vv. 21-23). Yahweh wants justice and a right ordering to life that makes sense of the celebrations (v. 24).

This proclamation of reversal on the Day of Yahweh influenced later prophets, poets, and preachers in Israelite and Judean tradition. The motif grew and developed, not only in Joel and Isaiah, but in Zephaniah and beyond. For a long time the cultic/festival setting remained a striking facet in its proclamation. Ultimately, more and more attention came to be paid to the manner of the punishment, the means of destruction. That, combined with the casting of this imminent Day into a hazy future as apocalyptic literature grew, led to a different emphasis in the use of this imagery. Throughout its development, however, the Day of the Lord continued to communicate fundamental truths about God's demand for justice, God's desire to see it at work among the people *now* and the need for worship to reflect a just order. Such preaching is as relevant and necessary today as it was in the time of Amos.

Application for Preaching and Teaching

Feast or Famine?
Amos 5:18-27
1 Thessalonians 5:1-11

[Amos's "Day of the Lord" involves a rejection of festive celebration because of injustices in society, but, as noted in the exegesis, the motif developed beyond Amos and found its way ultimately into early Christian writings. This sermon attempts to take into account the biblical "updating" of this theme as it is applied to contemporary life. It was preached in Canada the week before Advent Sunday, so in the States it would have landed on or near Thanksgiving . . . and that setting would work very well! This version attends rather more to exposition, with the expectation that hooks into local situations will be provided by preachers in their own settings.]

Introduction

Each year when Advent season comes we can count on certain things: the wreaths will be out, candles will be lit, carols will be sung. In many churches special services will be held, as the story of Advent—beginning with the expectations of the prophets and culminating in the birth of Jesus—will anticipate Christmas itself. It is a time of expectation and anticipation. Even before Advent, one can see Christmas decorations going up around town—and as my toddler says when he sees the lights, "There's Christmas!" The decorations are in the malls, and we're looking forward to family time: visits, food, gifts . . . basically, hedonism and gluttony! But, I'm here to tell you:

NO LIGHTS
NO CAROLS
NO GIFTS
NO TURKEY
NO TREE . . .
NO JOY!!!

Or, at least, this is how things would sound if we put ourselves in the shoes of those who heard Amos proclaim his famous "Day of the Lord."

This "Day" has its own history, and it recurs at several points in the Bible. But with Amos, we see it at its beginning—the first time it is used, so far as we know. As it is picked up, used, and adapted by other prophets and preachers in the Bible, it is transformed, so that each occurrence has its own "voice." Today, we focus on two of these voices: the voices of Amos and Paul, which give the first and one of the last appearances of the "Day of the Lord" motif in the Bible.

5:18-27. Amos was probably the earliest of the prophets to leave us a collection of his sermons in written form. He was active in Israel at a time when it and its sister state, Judah, were both enjoying a time of political and economic prosperity.

One of the key features of religious life in Amos's day were the pilgrimage festivals: times when you would leave your home, taking your sacrifices with you, and go to the temple, there to join in festive celebration and offer gifts to God. These were family times, times of joy and feasting, of community and fellowship. The "Big One" came in the fall, during the feast of ingathering, or feast of "booths" or "tabernacles," as it came to be called.

The opening chapters of Samuel, where Hannah prays for a son, take place in exactly this sort of setting. You may recall that when the old priest Eli saw her praying silently, he immediately thought she was tipsy. His assumption gives a good indication of the level of merriment at the time of festival!

This was the big binge, the let-your-hair-down-and-thank-God-that's-over celebration that marked the end of all the hard labor in the fields and vineyards. While you were bringing in the olives, the grapes, and gathering the late grains, at least you could wipe the sweat off your brow and know that soon it would be time to celebrate!

Enter Amos. *NO!* he cries, or rather proclaims on the Lord's behalf. This won't be a time of sweetness and light, of feasting and frolic. Rather, it will be a day of deep darkness, a day for worship to be rejected, a day when songs will be silenced.

Amos paints a terrifying word-picture for his hearers, worthy of any horror that Alfred Hitchcock could create. In the fields, a man encounters a lion and runs for his life, only to turn a corner and run into the claws and teeth of a bear. He manages to escape—how, he doesn't know—and arrives home. As he collapses in weary relief against the strong walls of his house, a waiting serpent bites him, and its lethal poison did what the lion's and bear's claws could not do. Death, says Amos, is inescapable.

Why this terror? Why famine rather than feast? Why darkness rather than light? Amos provides the answer. These people had turned their backs on a just society, had grown greedy, and in their greed had oppressed their neighbors. Their worship lacked integrity and was hollow. The plenty they wanted to enjoy was only for themselves, and not for the benefit of all God's people. Nor were their energies devoted to serving their Lord; rather, they did everything for themselves.

For Amos, God's spokesperson, the inevitable result of greed and oppression was the rejection of their festival "worship" of the Lord. No just God could tolerate such a situation or be honored by such service. The call goes out for a complete change of orientation: "But let justice roll down like waters, and righteousness like an everflowing stream."

Interlude

Not long after Amos announced the coming day of darkness—certainly within a generation—his words were fulfilled. The nation of Israel was destroyed, exiled far beyond Damascus. Many died. Those who survived lost their identity as aliens, far from their home.

We sometimes think that the problem with prophecy lies in its failure: what happens when some forecast does not come true? Seldom do we consider the equal and opposite "problem": what do you do with prophecies that do come true? Amos's words came true, and they were known to be prophecies of power, with their origin not in the imaginations of creatures, but in the heart of the Creator.

What to do with such powerful words? Here and there we see responses to the Day of the Lord: it was understood as a day of wrath when, without pity but in justice, God punished God's people. We see in various places efforts to understand what the continuing significance of the Day would be. This, in itself, was a prophetic task. And so the focus came to be on the results of the Day of the Lord, rather than its causes. The roots of the Day in the empty festivities of Israelites receded, but the idea of the Day of the Lord continued to grow and develop.

Paul (1 Thess 5:1-11)

One of the features of Amos's proclamation that lived on was the contrast between "darkness" and "light." Throughout the Bible, the light is a place of life; the dark, the night, is a time of evil and death.

We might not think of "Amos-in-the-New-Testament," but when we come to Paul's first preserved letter, that is exactly the way our thoughts should turn. We tend not to consider the New Testament's "Day of the Lord" in Old Testament terms. We think of it—if we think of it at all!—only in relationship to the future and unexpected return, the second coming, of Jesus. We are probably all aware of the debates that rage around *that* topic! But such debates, with their decidedly future orientation, miss important aspects of the New Testament "Day," aspects that our attention to Amos can help us recover.

Future concern was, already, a matter of anxiety for the early church, even here in our very oldest Christian writing. Paul attempts to address these fears by describing the coming "Day of the Lord" in terms of a "thief" (building on Jesus' words in Matt 24:42-44; Luke 12:39-40). Other figures of speech are used as well, as, for instance, birth pangs. One might think, in some situations, that vigilance removes the element of surprise. Every parent knows the sudden crisis that attends the announcement: "I think it's time to get to the hospital!" You wait, and wait, always expecting . . . but whenever the time arrives, it is always "all-of-a-sudden"!

The point Paul is making is not that vigilance removes surprise; that just does not happen. Rather, watching in vigilance affects life here-and-now. Here is where Amos's imagery of light and darkness comes into play. The quality of life exhibited by Amos's hearers was such that their "light" was to be plunged into darkness. So, Paul here urges his friends, "You are all children of the light and children of the day; we are not of the night or of darkness" (5:5). The consequence of this bears on lifestyle. They are not to be profligate, wasteful, or drunken. Rather, they live lives that are in keeping with the salvation that God has prepared through Jesus Christ.

Afterwords

Such is the impact and significance of the "Day of the Lord." It is not just about the dim, distant past (Amos), nor is it only about a hazy future (Paul). It is about living lives that honor God and make sense of our worship of God. Some final observations help bring this home.

The bottom line in the "Day of the Lord" is that God holds the initiative. It is a reminder again of who is the Creator and who is the creature. It is a reminder again that no matter how we plot, plan, or program, God can and will act sovereignly to bring honor to God's self. God is not honored when lives and liturgy do not connect. Amos proclaimed the rejection of both—life and service—in his day. God turned His back on His own people's religious observance.

The "Day of the Lord" is never simply a future event. Throughout the Old Testament, the "Day" is always just around the corner, and prophecies concerning it are for today. Amos, in his powerful proclamation, had no intention of providing fodder for speculating futurists. He wanted to communicate God's deep disappointment and outrage and the greedy feasting of the people. For Paul, too, matters are not just oriented to the future: rather, expectation of a coming day is intended to affect the quality of life lived now.

The "Day of the Lord" has more to do with action than belief. This has to do with ethics, morals, and patterns of behavior much more than it has to do with creeds or "right belief," as important as that may be.

We get so caught up in our debates about correct interpretation and using the right form of words. The "Day of the Lord" reminds us that all such energies are wasted—and bring no pleasure to God—if they are not matched by lives that are lived in the open, in the light.

As we build anticipation during Advent, as we see lights, buy gifts, sing carols, attend services, as we carry on with our festival observances, *this* is the challenge of the Day of the Lord. Do we just want the feast? Or do we want the "feast" to be just?

Notes

[1]C. F. Keil, *Minor Prophets*, Commentary on the Old Testament, trans. James Martin (Grand Rapids MI: Eerdmans, 1978) 287; Hans Walter Wolff, *Joel and Amos: A Commentary on the Books of the Prophets Joel and Amos*, trans. W. Janzen et al. (Philadelphia: Fortress, 1977) 256. F. I. Andersen and D. N. Freedman; *Amos: A New Translation with Introduction and Commentary*, Anchor Bible (New York: Doubleday, 1989) 24: 522; Shalom M. Paul, *Amos: A Commentary on the Book of Amos*, Hermeneia (Minneapolis: Fortress, 1991) 186.

[2]William Rainey Harper, *A Critical and Exegetical Commentary on Amos and Hosea*, International Critical Commentary (Edinburgh: T. & T. Clark, 1905) 132; James Luther Mays, *Amos: A Commentary*, Old Testament Library (London and Philadelphia: SCM/Westminster, 1969) 105.

[3]Mays, 105, thinks there has been irreparable damage.

[4]Paul, 190, argues that this is the true sense of the Hebrew original.

[5]Andersen and Freedman, 523.

[6]For graphic illustration of these practices, see O. Keel, *The Symbolism of the Biblical World: Ancient Near Eastern Iconography and the Book of Psalms* (New York: Seabury, 1978) 307-55. Cf. also J. B. Pritchard, *The Ancient Near East in Pictures Relating to the Old Testament*, 2d ed. (Princeton: Princeton University Press, 1969) 797.

[7]Paul, 193, note 5, following M. Astour.

[8]Cf. Psalm 29, esp. 29:3, generally agreed to have similar echoes.

[9]Andersen and Freedman, 530.

[10]Two excellent illustrations, roughly contemporary with Amos, of gods being carried in festal procession and into exile, can be found in *ANED*, nos. 537-38. See also the accompanying text, 314-15.

[11]Mays, 103.

[12]Ibid., 146-47.

[13]Douglas Stuart, *Hosea-Jonah*, Word Biblical Themes (Dallas: Word, 1989) 385; Andersen and Freedman, 821.

[14]For survey of scholarly work on this theme, see esp. Ladislave Cerny, *The Day of Yahweh and Some Relevant Problems* (Prague: Nákladen Filosofické Fakulty University Karlovy, 1948); Meir Weiss, "The Origin of the 'Day of the Lord'—Reconsidered," *Hebrew Union College Annual* 37 (1966): 29-72; Hans M. Barstad, *The Religious Polemics of Amos: Studies in the Preaching of Amos 2, 7B-8; 4,1-13; 5,1-27; 6,4-7; 8,14*, Supplements to Velus Testamentum (Leiden: E.J. Brill, 1984) 4:89-93, 97-103; K. J. Cathcart, "Day of Yahweh," *The Anchor Bible Dictionary*, ed. David Noel Freedman (New York: Doubleday, 1992) 84-85.

[15]Gerhard von Rad, *The Theology of Israel's Prophetic Traditions*, Old Testament Theology (1965) 2:119-25.

[16]Wolff, 256; Paul, 184; and Stuart, 353.

[17]Mays, 104.

Chapter Seven

"The Search"

Amos 6:1-14

R. Wayne Stacy

Background

My Hermeneutic

To call a document "scripture" is to say at least three things about it. Of course, it is to say that the document is old. Scripture is not composed by the community that hallows it. It must go through a "proving period" before it is installed as scripture. Amos did not start out one day from Tekoa and say to himself: "You know, I think I'll write a book of the Bible today so that years from now folk can study it in their winter Bible studies." No, it is crucial to remember that the Bible was a "word of God" to someone else before it was the "Word of God" to us.

Scriptural documents are "time-sensitive" documents. They were written at a particular time to a particular people in particular circumstances, all of which must be analyzed and understood if the documents are to be comprehensible to us today. That is to say, we must know what it meant before we can know what it means. Historical analysis of biblical documents, therefore, is not optional; it is necessary if we are to hear a word of God for us today.

Moreover, to call a document "scripture" is to claim it as authoritative. Somehow or other, in ways still fraught with mystery, when we read this document we call "scripture," we hear the voice of God addressing us. Therefore, it is not just a "text." Text implies that the document is merely a curiosity, an artifact for study, but not something that makes demands of its inquirer. To call something "scripture" means that to a greater or lesser degree it stands in judgment over us.

To call something "scripture" is to claim it for the community of faith. In other words, it is the church's book. The "voice" that addresses us in scripture does not just make demands on us as individuals; it calls us to responsible community. It is not your scripture or my scripture, it is our scripture. That is why it is altogether appropriate, and perhaps even necessary, for the study of the scripture to culminate in the proclamation of the scripture, for it calls us into responsible community.

In light of the preceding ideas, in what follows we will attempt to set the scripture in its context by offering an exegesis of Amos 6:1-14. This we will do first by setting our passage in its historical context (What in the world was going on when Amos spoke these words?). Then we will set the text in its literary context (What is the literary structure of 6:1-14, and how does Amos 6:1-14 fit into the rest of the book?). Then in an expositional section, we will comment briefly on several exegetical matters of significance for interpretation and, consequently, preaching.

Finally, we will set the text in its theological context (What is the "Word of God" in this text; that is, what is Amos teaching us about the way and work and will of God in the world that was true then and is true still?). From this last analysis (the theological context), we will attempt to set the text in *our* context by isolating the governing theological theme for Amos 6:1-14, which will then serve as the theme of our sermon.

The Historical Context

The period in which Amos prophesied is known as Israel's "silver age," as distinct from its "golden age" when David reigned. Amos's ministry probably dates to the period 760–750 B.C. This was a time of tremendous prosperity and power. Jeroboam's military conquests had expanded the frontiers of Israel to a point where they nearly rivaled the great Davidic monarchy. In the north, Israel's territory extended as far as Lebo-Hamath (cf. 2 Kgs 14:25), and in the south Israel laid claim to land all the way to the Arabah (cf. Amos 6:14 where the phrase "from Lebo-hamath to Wadi Arabah" defines Israel's territory under Jeroboam). This territorial expansion, secured through a series of alliances with foreign powers, most especially Assyria, gave rise to unparalleled trade and commerce in Israel.[1] This in turn resulted in the development of a small, but extremely affluent merchant class that enjoyed the "good life" at the expense of the poor, working class.

Archaeological excavations in Samaria have documented the opulence and ease of the upper classes in Israel during Amos's time. Not surprisingly, Israel's wealthy interpreted their good fortune as the blessing of God. They built lavish shrines and conducted elaborate rituals for the purpose of showing their gratitude to God for God's many favors. There was no shortage of "religion" in Israel during this period (cf. Amos 4–5), and it was all designed to express praise to God for God's "good sense" in blessing so worthy a people as Israel. How easy it is to make the transition from "praise God from whom all blessings flow" to "praise blessings in which our virtue doth show." With their military alliances firmly in place, their economic prosperity assured, and their religious "guarantors" solidly ensconced, Israel felt secure and satisfied.

Into that climate of "conspicuous consumption" entered Amos the prophet, hurling his defiant words in the face of the greatest power of the period. His message was chillingly clear: security is to be found only in God! Israel, Amos asserts, has substituted economic and political security for the only true security—covenant faithfulness to God—and has substituted the trappings of religion for the essence of religion— honesty, integrity, and justice. The message of Amos was memorable, not just because of what he said, but because of the way he said it. To that we turn now.

The Literary Context

Our passage, 6:1-14, falls within the larger section, 5:18–6:14, which can be designated "The Two Woes." The first "woe" oracle (which is *hôy* in Hebrew) is found in 5:18-27 and deals with the concept of the "Day of the LORD" (*yom Yhwh*). Specifically, the oracle is Amos's reinterpretation of the well-known "Day of the LORD" prophecy, the prophet reversing the usual meaning of the imagery. Typically the Day of the Lord was understood as a day when Yahweh would punish Israel's enemies and restore Israel to its former glory (see Isa 34–35). It was regarded as a great and glorious day for Israel. Amos, however, reverses that imagery and instead defines the Day of the Lord as a day of judgment upon Israel for exchanging ritual ceremony for faithfulness to the covenant: "Is not the day of the LORD darkness, not light, and gloom with no brightness in it?" (5:20)

Our passage is the second "woe" oracle, 6:1-14, in which the prophet pronounces judgment upon Israel for its garish and opulent lifestyle, a lifestyle that dishonors God and debases the poor. That these two "woe" oracles belong together is evinced by the fact that both begin with the formulaic expression "Alas for you/those who . . . ," followed by a description of the doomed behavior (compare 5:18 with 6:1). Also, following the "woe" oracle in each section is a "declaration of despising" in which God, speaking through the prophet, declares hatred for the particular behavior that has evoked God's ire (cf. 5:21— "I hate, I despise your festivals, and I take no delight in your solemn assemblies"—and 6:8—"I abhor the pride of Jacob, and hate his strongholds").

In short, the formal affinities between these two sections indicate that they are "companion oracles" intended to interact with and augment each other. If one is looking for a conceptual framework with which to distinguish them, it could be said that the first "woe" (5:18-27) pronounces God's judgment upon Israel's sacred life, while the second "woe" (6:1-14) declares that God has cursed Israel's secular life.

A word about "woes" may be in order. Woe (*hoy*) oracles were a stylized way of pronouncing a curse upon a person, a class of persons, or a nation. A "woe" is the opposite of a "blessing" (compare Isa 5:11-13). As in the case of a blessing, a woe both declares and effects the condition it asserts. It does what it says. (This is the background for Jesus' use of the "woe" oracle in his so-called "Sermon on the Level Plain" in Luke 6 where, in good prophetic fashion, he declares: "Woe to you rich, for you have been paid in full" [my translation]).

As to the internal structure of 6:1-14, as noted above, this passage, as was the case with the first "woe" oracle (5:18-27), falls into two divisions: the "woe" oracle (6:1-7) and the companion "hate" oracle (6:8-14). There are also several other tell-tale indications that 6:1-14 forms a distinctive literary unit. For example, Amos will employ a device known as "inclusio" to delineate, as it were, the literary boundaries of an oracle and to instruct the reader/hearer that the material contained within should be interpreted as a unit. Inclusio is the practice of repeating a word or an idea at the beginning and ending of literary unit in order to tip off the reader that it should be treated as a whole. For example, in 6:1 Amos pronounces a woe on the "notables of the first of the nations."

The key word is "first" (*rosh*), a reference to Israel's false pride over its international status at the time. Then, in verse 7, Amos will again mention his key word "first," only this time, he declares that Israel, which wanted to be considered "first" among the nations, will indeed be "first": "They shall now be the *first* of those to go into the exile." The two references to "first" delineate the boundaries of the "woe" oracle and indicate that everything in between these two verses should be taken as God's "curse" (woe) upon Israel's false pride and false sense of security.

The same thing can be observed in the "hate" oracle (6:8-14). This time, instead of the word "first," Amos employs the formulaic phrase "says the LORD, the God of hosts." In 6:8 Yahweh declares that he "hates" Jacob's pride, swearing an oath by God's self (the highest thing God knows to swear by) to punish Israel for its arrogance. Then, to add solemnity to the oath, Amos adds the formula: "says the LORD, the God of hosts." At the end of the "hate" oracle, Amos brackets the entire oath of promised punishment together by means of the repeated formula: "says the LORD, the God of hosts" (6:14), indicating that everything that falls in between should be "included" (cf. "inclusio") together as comprising a single literary unit.

Therefore, we feel justified in treating Amos 6:1-14 as a unit. The passage can be characterized as a "woe" oracle with its accompanying "hate" oracle, which is in the form of an oath that Yahweh swears by God's self and in which Yahweh declares the intention to punish Israel, especially Israel's elite upper class, for its pride, its callous treatment of the poor, and its false sense of security.

Exposition

Although many excellent verse-by-verse commentaries on the book of Amos are available, that kind of analysis is neither necessary nor particularly useful for our purposes. The purpose of this study is to understand the message of the text in its context and then to bring that forward and say it again sermonically here in our context. Yet, a few issues in chapter 6 require some comment if we are to understand Amos's message. We take them up in turn.

6:1. "at ease in Zion . . . Some scholars have suggested that because Amos's prophetic commission was to prophesy in the North (Israel), the reference to "Zion" is secondary, added later to make the book of Amos more "inclusive" of Israel as a whole, including the southern kingdom of Judah. Remember that Amos was himself from the South, and so it is not surprising that he would address some of his prophetic preachments to his own people. In the eighth century B.C., moreover, Samaria, not "Zion" (Jerusalem) was the center of religious and political life in Israel, and so Amos, a Judean, utters his prophecies in Samaria. But because all parts of Israel stand together in the judgment of God, Amos includes "Zion" in his indictment.

Also in verse 1 is the issue of who the "notables of the first of the nations" are. Specifically, are there three different groups mentioned here or just one inclusive group of all Israelites? In Hebrew thought, a phenomenon called "parallelism" is crucial to the interpretation of a poetic or prophetic message. Parallelism is of three types: (1) "Regular" parallelism is a poetic way of stating something and then restating it with slightly different language. (2) "Antithetical" parallelism states something and then states the exact opposite of it. (3) "Synthetic" parallelism states something and then seeks to build upon or enlarge the earlier statement by adding to it another statement that furthers its meaning.

Is Amos employing regular parallelism or synthetic parallelism in his three statements in verse 1: (1) "Alas for those who are at ease in

Zion"; (2) "and for those who feel secure on Mount Samaria"; and (3) "the notables of the first of the nations, to whom the house of Israel resorts"? That is, is there only one group in view (Israelites, north and south), or are there three groups in view (Judean, Israelites, and "the notables")?

If Amos is using regular parallelism, then the "notables" are the leading officials of Samaria, just as are those "at ease in Zion" and "secure on Mount Samaria" to whom the "house of Israel resorts" to beg favors and to secure their meager subsistence. If Amos is applying synthetic parallelism, the "notables" are probably the Assyrians "to whom the house of Israel resorts" in order to secure themselves with military alliances. Both explanations are plausible, but the former has in its favor one overriding factor: the inclusio with verse 7. If the "notables" are the Assyrians, then the ironic inclusio of verse 7 is lost: "You wanted to be first? Well, you can be first all right, first to go into exile!" But if the "notables of the first of the nations" is a further reference to Israelites, then the irony is intact.

6:2. "Calneh," "Hamath the great," and "Gath of the Philistines" are references to victorious military campaigns under Shalmaneser III of Assyria, mentioned here because they had become legendary by this time. Amos sarcastically derides Israel's false pride by suggesting that Israel's meager military might is no match for Assyria's, and so Israel is foolish to put its trust in armies and military hubris.

6:3. "The evil day" is a reference to the "Day of the LORD," which was the subject of the first "woe" (5:18-27). Amos again turns the image of the Day of the Lord from one of jubilation to one of judgment. Note also the ironic use of language in the antithetical use of the verbs "put away" and "bring near." They hope to "put away" the evil day of judgment, when in fact they are only "bringing near" the time of violence.

6:4-6. What follows here is a "mini-woe" detailing the opulent, carefree lifestyle of Samaria's powerful and wealthy. It is a satirical exposé of the "conspicuous consumption" that had so corrupted Israel's upper class. Amos, with sardonic delight, details their insatiable taste for "the finer things," everything from ivory inlaid bedding to gourmet gorgings of chateaubriand.

One of the most interesting references is in verse 6. Amos chastises the elite for drinking wine in bowls and anointing themselves with the finest (literally "first," *rosh*) oils. Wine and oil were widely regarded as the two most pleasure-bringing commodities, reserved exclusively for the wealthy. In Israel's wisdom literature, oil and wine are routinely paired as descriptions of the "good life." Similarly, the abstinence from joy and revelry during periods of mourning is characterized by the refraining from the use of oil and wine.

This association was, no doubt, the background for John's enigmatic reference to these two commodities in Revelation 6:6, when one of the four horsemen, specifically the one who brings famine, declares: "A quart of wheat for a day's pay, and three quarts of barley for a day's pay, but do not damage the olive oil and the wine." Like Amos before him, John also recognized that in difficult times, the poor grope for subsistence while the rich enjoy their luxuries.

6:7. "and the revelry of the loungers shall pass away" . . . After describing the depraved debauchery of the wealthy in terms of a banquet at which the participants luxuriate on ivory couches, drink wine from bowls, cover themselves with fine oil, and sing idle songs for their own amusement, in verse 7 Amos gives the image a macabre twist. The word he uses as "revelry" is actually *mirzach* in Hebrew. The *mirzach* was a funeral feast at which the participants, through eating and drinking dedicated to a god, insured the security of the deceased loved one after death.[2] In excavations at Palmyra, the *mirzach* was actually performed with the very kinds of activities Amos depicts here: reclining on couches, eating, drinking, and anointing with oil.[3] With macabre irony, Amos declares that in the wealthy's endless banqueting they were unwittingly participating in their own *mirzach!*

6:8. The "hate" oracle begins with an oath formula that employs the phrase "says the LORD the God of hosts," which is repeated at verse 14 to form an inclusio. The use of the oath stresses the certainty of the coming judgment and punishment upon Israel.[4] The phrase "pride of Jacob" encapsulates the essential nature of Israel's sin, that it attempted to secure itself through its own devises, apart from the trust in God that had created Israel as a nation and sustained it as a people. It also probably repeats a slogan current at the time that captured in a phrase Israel's national hubris. The "city" that will be delivered up is Samaria.

6:9-11. From the "macro-visioned" perspective of the destruction of Samaria, Amos now moves in to give the judgment a human face. We are taken inside a "typical Samarian house" to view "up close and personal" what God's punishment of Israel will mean.

6:12-13. By means of two rhetorical questions that demand the answer "no," Amos drives home the folly of Israel's pride. "Do horses run on rocks?" he asks. The answer, of course, is "no," for to do so would ruin their hooves. "Does one plow the sea with oxen?" Of course not. The question itself is absurd, and so is Israel's current course of action. They have tried to secure themselves through economic privilege, military achievements, and foreign alliances, and yet Amos describes all their so-called "achievements" to be "nothing" ("you who rejoice in Lo-debar"—literally "no thing").

The specific historical references of "Lo-debar" and "Karnaim" are to military excursions into the Transjordan during the reign of Jeroboam II. The Israelites apparently took great pride in conquering these two cities. Amos's sarcasm is biting when he suggests that Israel's military achievements are well-named: Lo-debar, "no-thing." In a marvelous alliteration, Shalom Paul describes Amos's indictment of Israel's arrogance with the sentence: "For Amos their panegyrical preening pride pompously precedes their precipitous fall."

6:14. The form of verse 14 is accurately translated, but not the force. The Hebrew delays the impact of Amos's words until the last possible moment. Actually, it says: "But lo, I am raising up, says the LORD, the God of hosts, *against you* a nation." Amos allows the hearer/reader to ponder whether the verb "raising up" is positive or negative until the moment when he lets the other shoe drop . . . "a nation." Though Amos never divulges the identity of that "nation" by means of which God will punish Israel for its false pride and false security, we know that nation was Assyria whose eventual domination of Israel was total and complete, "from Lebo-hamath to Wadi Arabah."

The Theological Context

The difficulty in reading Amos and trying to bring his message forward and say it here is to avoid the temptation of using the text merely as a jeremiad (perhaps I should say "amosiad") against wealth per se and allowing the sermon to degenerate into a diatribe against the rich. Such an approach misses the point on two counts. First, it is inappropriate because nowhere in the scriptures is wealth treated as evil intrinsically. As C. S. Lewis said: "Evil is a parasite." That is to say, evil has no independent life. Everything bad is something good that has been bent, misshaped, twisted toward some inappropriate end. The biblical perspective is that God created all things and pronounced them "good." Evil, then, is the result of misdirecting or twisting God's essentially good creation toward some end not originally envisioned by the Creator. That, of course, is true of wealth. Wealth per se is not evil; rather, treating what was originally intended by God to be a means as an end constitutes the evil.

It is also inappropriate merely to vilify the wealthy in this text because to do so would be to settle for a shallow, surface reading of Amos. Wealth per se does not concern Amos. People of wealth (or poverty, for that matter) can be either saints or sinners, but nothing in either wealth or poverty necessarily makes them so. No, Amos is after "bigger fish" than that! His concern is the idolatry that reliance upon wealth can degenerate into when the people of God forget that they are God's people and instead put their trust and find their security apart from God. Robin Scroggs is right on target when he defines sin as "the attempt to secure the self apart from God."[5]

The real issue for Amos, as the preceding analysis has made clear, is the deeper issue of security: "Alas for those who are at ease in Zion, and for those who feel secure on Mount Samaria." Amos opposes all illegitimate attempts to secure the self apart from relationship with the God who alone secures us. Amos takes no pleasure in the persecution and humiliation of Israel or its wealthy upper class. He is rather issuing a "wake-up call" (see 9:11-15).

Charles Talbert rightly understands the redemptive role that persecution and suffering can have when he says:

The importance of rejection, persecution, suffering, and the threat of death in the process of spiritual growth is that each entails the possibility of the loss of something which the self either holds dear or is tempted to grasp: one is threatened with the loss of economic security, of status, reputation, or life itself. Circumstances remove the possibility of one's holding to any of these real or potential false gods . . . Rejection or persecution shatter real or potential idols and allows God to draw one to himself alone.[6]

And so we must resist the temptation to bring this text forward merely as a diatribe against wealth. Instead I choose to address the more substantive issue of the book of Amos and the real issue lurking behind the doom and gloom of chapter 6, a question that hovers over all Amos says: Where do we find our ultimate security? In the nearly 2,800 intervening years, not much has changed, really. This is our question too. Whatever distances we obtain between Amos's world and ours, here is a question that can still be posed with profit to a contemporary audience. The governing theological theme of the sermon, then, will be: Because we were made not just *by* God but *for* God, our ultimate security is found only in relationship with God.

Application for Preaching and Teaching

"The Search"
Amos 6:1-14

In his book *Where the Sidewalk Ends,* Shel Silverstein has written a haunting little poem that he calls "The Search." It goes like this:

> I went to find the pot of gold
> That's waiting where the rainbow ends.
> I searched and searched and searched and searched
> And searched and searched, and then—
> There it was, deep in the grass,
> Under an old and twisty bough.
> It's mine, it's mine, it's mine at last . . .
> What do I search for now?

Now, I understand this man! The lure of the discovery of that which will finally make one "secure," the proverbial "pot of gold" at the end of the rainbow, the feeling that one has finally "arrived" (where we are not sure, but we know we are not "there" now)—all of these can be consuming, literally. Indeed, in antiquity this search is often pictured as a gnawing, insatiable appetite, a "hunger" that cannot be sated.

There's an old, old story, widely traveled, about a hermit who stumbled onto a cave in which there was hidden an enormous treasure. The hermit, being old and wise of years, realized what he had discovered and immediately took to his heels and ran from the cave as fast as he could. But as he was running, he came upon three brigands who stopped him and inquired as to what he was fleeing. "I'm fleeing the Devil!" he said. Curious, they said: "Show us." Protesting all the way, he took them to the cave where he had found the treasure. "Here," said the hermit, "is death which was running after me."

Well, the three thought the old man was touched and sent him on his way. Gleefully reveling in their newfound treasure, they determined that one of them should be dispatched to bring back provisions, lest they leave their treasure to others. One volunteered, thinking to himself that while in town, he would poison the food and kill his rivals, possessing the treasure for himself. But while he was away, the other two had been thinking as well! They decided to kill their comrade when he returned and divide the spoils between themselves. This they did, and then they settled down to eat their food and celebrate their successful cabal. Their banquet turned out to be a funeral feast, however, for when the poison hit their stomachs, they too expired, leaving the treasure as they had found it.

That is one of the oldest pictures of greed we have. It lurks in caves; it deals in death. But the search goes on, and the hunger is unabated. And like a man looking for the market where life is sold, we run all over town with a fistful of twenty-dollar bills saying, "Hey, could I buy a . . . " "No, sorry, we don't sell homes here. We can sell you a house." "No, sorry, we don't sell love here. We can sell you a companion for the night." "No, sorry, we don't sell any time. I have a good clock here, but not a tick of time."

The lure of "the search" can be consuming. That elusive goal of "financial independence" got millions to watch the halftime of the Super Bowl recently. No, Elvis was not performing. Rather, the draw was Ed McMahon and Dick Clark cruising America in the Publisher's Clearing House Prize Patrol van looking for the house where they would make someone an instant millionaire. The prize would be awarded on live TV during halftime of the Super Bowl, and millions of Americans were peering out their windows saying: "Is that a van I see coming down our street?"

This is not a new phenomenon. Israel was engaged in such a search in the eight century B.C. when the prophet Amos came along and called the whole enterprise into question. It was the "silver age" of Israel during the reign of Jeroboam II when the search began in earnest. Under Jeroboam, Israel enjoyed nearly unparalleled prosperity, power, and prestige. Jeroboam's military conquests had expanded the frontiers to a point where Israel's holdings nearly rivaled those of the great Davidic monarchy. "From the entrance of Hamath to the Brook of the Arabah" was the proud slogan of the day. Here in North Carolina we say "from Manteo to Murphy." You get the idea. In order to further secure this new expansionism, Jeroboam negotiated a series of alliances with foreign powers, chiefly Assyria, and the resulting *pax Jeroboam* gave rise to unparalleled trade and commerce in Israel.

Israel enjoyed "the good life" under Jeroboam, and the affluent upper class people who were the chief beneficiaries of this unprecedented economic and military security celebrated their good fortune with "conspicuous consumption," flaunting an opulent lifestyle that included garish banquets and endless revelry. Under Jeroboam Israel had "arrived," there was "ease in Zion" and "security in Samaria"—but not for everyone. Israel's poor, working class did not share in the blessings of the rich, and the gap between the "haves" and the "have-nots" grinned ghoulishly.

Enter Amos. Railing at the injustice and exploitation of Israel's wealthy against the poor, Amos hurled defiant words in the face of the "notables of the first of the nations": "You who trample the poor and take from him exactions of wheat . . . who afflict the righteous, who take bribes, and turn aside the needy in the gate . . . Thus saith the

LORD, the God of hosts, I will pass through your midst, and it's not for a social call"—or words to that effect.

Amos is not merely after a "redistribution of wealth," however. Israel's problem is more basic than that.

> Alas for those who are at ease in Zion, and to those who feel secure on Mount Samaria . . . they shall be the first to go into exile, and the revelry of the loungers [on banquet couches] shall pass away.

Israel's problem is not just greed or even exploitation of fellow Israelites, as bad as that is. Rather, the people of Israel have attempted to secure themselves apart from God! Wealth per se is not the problem. If it were, then merely redistributing the wealth from the rich to the poor would solve nothing and would, in fact, work to the detriment of the poor, making them the new recipients of the "evil stuff."

There is nothing necessarily or intrinsically evil in wealth, anymore than there is anything necessarily or intrinsically virtuous in poverty. People of wealth or poverty can be either saints or sinners, but nothing in their economic status as such makes them so. As C. S. Lewis has put it: "Evil is a parasite." That is, evil has no independent life. Everything bad is something essentially good that has been bent, misshaped, or twisted toward some inappropriate end. The biblical perspective is that God created all things and pronounced them "good." No, Amos was not merely concerned with a redistribution of wealth. He has "bigger fish to fry" than that!

Now do not misunderstand me. I am not saying that "rich" and "poor" are the same, only relative. I remind you, by the world's standards, everyone reading this page or hearing these words is "rich." The vast majority of the citizens of this country step on scales every day. The biggest single "party affiliation" in this country is neither Democrat nor Republican; it is "weight watchers," a problem most of the world could not understand. Amos never in his wildest dreams envisioned a world where the quality of life even remotely approached the one you and I enjoy. That is not what he meant.

Nor am I saying that we should not care about economic justice. In a "world without borders," anyone anywhere who is starving is my neighbor starving! But a jeremiad (perhaps I should say "amosiad") against the "rich," always careful to define "rich" as someone other than me, hardly does justice to the prophet's words. No, Amos has in mind the idolatry of treating as an end that which was originally intended to be merely a means: "Woe to those at ease in Zion and secure in Samaria." Saint Augustine once put it this way: "We enjoy those things that were meant only to be used, and we use those things that were meant to be enjoyed." And so we go through life getting our advanced degrees, earning our salaries, driving our cars, paying our mortgages, believing all the while that this establishes who we really are only to be reminded when we least expect it what we have always really known: We are all just a stroke or a tumor away from finding out who we *really* are.

One of my favorite movies was a story simply called *Julia*. It was about a friendship between a woman named Julia and the famous playwright Lillian Hellman. My favorite scene in the movie occurred one night when Lillian Hellman (played by Jane Fonda) was sitting out by the fire on the beach talking with her literary mentor, Dashiell Hammett (played by Jason Robards), creator of the "Sam Spade" character and author of such mystery novels as *The Maltese Falcon* and *The Thin Man*. Lillian had just published her first play, her famous *The Little Foxes*, and was for the first time realizing some fame and financial independence.

Sitting there by the firelight, thoughts of greatness fluttered up in her head, and she turned to Dashiell Hammett and said:

> Dash, do you think it would be frivolous of me to buy a mink coat with some of the money from my play? You know, I've never had much money, and I've always wanted a mink coat. I can just imagine walking into one of those posh New York writers' parties, all the big names there, wearing my new mink and having everyone in the place turn in chorus, look at me and say: "Why, that's Lillian Hellman. She's somebody!"

Hammett, stirring around in the coals and never looking at her, said:

Lilly, if you want a coat, buy a coat. God knows you've got the money now. But don't think for a moment that it has anything to do with writing. It's just a coat, Lilly. That's all. Just a coat.

The problem with wealth is not that it is intrinsically evil; rather, it seduces us into thinking that it can give what only God can give: security. "It's mine, it's mine, it's mine at last . . . what do I search for now?" That was Israel's problem, and in the nearly 2,800 intervening years it is surprising how little has changed. We still think that we can secure ourselves apart from God, but just like Israel's hollow pride in its economic and political and military clout, all our efforts at "independence" from God only serve to demonstrate just how impotent we really are outside of our relationship with God. The reason is not difficult to see: we were made not just by God but for God. God is the "fuel" on which we were designed to run, and should we try to run our lives on anything else, like Israel we discover that it will never work.

"Do horses run on rocks? Does one plow the sea with oxen?" To reject our absolute dependence on God in the search for security is to cut the cord that alone gives us our very lives. To find our security in anything other than our trust in God is not "salvation." Rather it is "damnation!"

Can you imagine Shakespeare's character Hamlet stopping in the middle of Shakespeare's famous play and saying: "Alright, alright, Will. I get the idea. I'll take it from here. I don't need you to write lines for me anymore." Would Hamlet have thereby discovered his "true self-hood?" Of course not! That would not be Hamlet's "salvation"; it would be his "destruction," for Hamlet, prince of Denmark, only exists in the creative imagination of William Shakespeare, and to seek to find his identity outside of and apart from that relationship is self-destruction.

So it is with you and me. We were made for God. God "thought us up" like characters in a play. There is no life; there is no security outside of that life-giving relationship with God! In the Old Testament we call that "covenant." In the New Testament we call it "gospel." Call it what you will, it is a "wake-up call."

Hear Amos: "Nothing—not wealth, not power, not position—Lo-debar, 'no-thing' can supply what you really seek. Because what you want, what you really want only God can give."

I searched and searched and searched and searched
And searched and searched, and then,
There it was, deep in the grass,
Under an old and twisty bough.
It's mine, it's mine, it's mine at last . . .
What do I search for now?

Fred Craddock, retired professor of preaching at Emory University, tells a story about playing hide-and-seek as a child. His family lived on a farm and did not have much money. Hide-and-seek did not cost anything, and it was something the kids could play.

You know how the game goes. Someone is "It." Whoever is "It" has to hide his eyes and count to 100. When he gets to 100, he says, "Here I come, ready or not." And then "It" looks high and low for those who have hidden. Then when she finds one, she says, "I found you!" and then races back to the "home base"—usually a tree or something—tags it three times, and then the person who is found becomes "It," and the game starts all over again. Simple.

Well, when Craddock's sister was "It," she cheated. Oh, she would start out honest enough: "1, 2, 3, 4, . . ." Then, when she thought no one was watching, she'd skip a bunch of numbers: "97, 98, 99, 100. Here I come, ready or not!" But Craddock had a way to beat her. He was much younger and smaller, and so he had a favorite place to hide where she could not find him. It was under the front porch steps. It was such a tight squeeze that no one else would even try it; but because he was so little, he could do it.

He would hear her counting: "97, 98, 99, 100; here I come, ready or not!" And out she went across the yard, out in the back, in the barn, out of the barn, in the corn crib, she could not find him! She looked everywhere! Once, she got close to the steps. Craddock thought she had found him. But she just sat down on the steps to rest, right over the top of where he was hiding. He started giggling and thought he would give it away, but he did not. He thought to himself: "She'll never find me. She'll never find me." Then it occurred to him: "She'll *never* find me!"

So Craddock stuck out a toe. She came by the steps, saw his toe, and said: "Uh oh, I found you!" She ran back to the tree, touched it three times, and said: "You're it!" He came out from under the steps, brushed off his clothes, and said: "Ah shucks! You *found* me!"

Now, why would he do that? What did he want? What did he really want? The very same thing as *you*. Isn't that true?

Notes

[1] Jeroboam II was a member of the royal house of Jehu, the same Jehu who is depicted on the Black Obelisk as paying tribute to the Assyrian king, Shalmaneser III. An inscription on the Obelisk says that Jehu presented Shalmaneser with tribute gifts and a staff of the king's hand. It is thought that this "staff" symbolized Jehu's placing of Israel under the aegis and protection of the Assyrian monarch, thus insuring Jehu and his descendents of Assyria's protection should a foreign nation ever attempt to invade. In one of history's great ironies, Assyria itself would invade Israel, with Samaria falling to its former ally in 722 B.C. See John H. Hayes, *Amos, The Eighth-Century Prophet: His Times and His Preching* (Nashville: Abingdon, 1988) 17ff.

[2] See Shalom M. Paul, *Amos*, Hermeneia, ed. Frank Moore Cross (Minneapolis: Augsburg Fortress, 1991) 210ff.

[3] Ibid., 212.

[4] Oaths were taken very seriously in the ancient Near East; indeed, even rash statements and ill-considered oaths carried obligations; cf. Lev 5:1-4; Judg 11:29ff. Gary V. Smith, *Amos: A Commentary* (Grand Rapids MI: Zondervan, 1989) 194.

[5] Robin Scroggs, *Paul for a New Day* (Philadelphia: Fortress, 1977) 5ff. Though this phrase is never used by Scroggs, it accurately gathers up his emphasis and is at the heart of the biblical view of sin.

[6] Charles Talbert, *Reading Luke: A Literary and Theological Commentary on the Third Gospel* (New York: Crossroads, 1986) 107.

Chapter Eight

"Never Again"

Amos 7:1-9

Cecil P. Staton, Jr.

Background

Structure

Amos 7:1–8:3 presents four visions of God's judgment upon Israel, the first three of which we will discuss in this chapter. The four visions—found in 7:1-3, 4-6, 7-9, and 8:1-3—are interrupted by the narrative of 7:10-17, which describes Amos's encounter with Amaziah, the priest of Bethel. Each vision begins with the phrase, "This is what the Lord GOD (or "he") showed me." In the first two visions, the prophet recounts some act of judgment upon Israel. This is followed by the prayer/intervention of the prophet. Following the prophetic intercession and at the last minute, Yahweh relents and Israel is forgiven. " 'It shall not be,' says Yahweh" (7:3, 6).

In the third and fourth visions, there is no equivalent to the judgment by locusts (v. 1) or fire (v. 4), and the prophetic intercession is missing. Instead, Amos is asked to describe what he sees. A plumb line or a basket of ripe summer fruit symbolizes Israel's crookedness and rottenness. Now Amos stands silent while Yahweh declares what are among the most frightening words from the mouth of God in all of scripture: "never again." Israel is beyond hope. A disastrous end will not be averted. Though the Lord God has relented in the past, Israel's actions have now set the nation on a course that will lead to its destruction. "The end has come upon my people Israel; I will never again pass them by" (8:2).

Text

7:1-3. First vision: a locust plague averted. The first two of the three visions begin with, "This is what the Lord GOD (*Adonai Elohim*) showed me" (7:1, 4). The third vision simply uses the third person form of the verb, "he showed me" (v. 7). The verb literally means "he caused me to see," thus suggesting that the prophet experienced a vision or saw some object that became a symbol of Yahweh's judgment upon Israel.

In the first vision, Amos is shown the formation of a locust plague (see Joel 1-2 for another description of a horrible locust plague). This occurs at a most inopportune time, just in time to destroy a whole season's work ("at the time the latter growth began to sprout"). The message was clear to the prophet. Just as the locusts had devoured the crop, so the Lord God would destroy Israel. Having watched as the locusts finished their destruction, the prophet rushed to speak, "O Lord God, forgive I beg you! How can Jacob stand? He is so small."

This text is revealing. Amos is frequently described as a prophet of judgment. Moreover, the words he was called to proclaim were difficult, harsh, unpopular words to speak. Amos, however, did not speak them without compassion and hope. Like Abraham who heard God's plans for Sodom and Gomorrah and offered intercession (Gen 18:16ff) and Moses who sought God's forgiveness for the "stiffnecked" children of Israel (Exod 33), so now Amos intercedes for "little/small" Israel. The word can mean "little" or "indifferent" and often refers to a young child. Amos's plea is that Israel is too insignificant to stand before God. Surely the Lord God must "pardon, forgive" Israel lest she fall before such destruction.

For now Amos has the power to restrain even God. "Yahweh relented concerning this: 'It shall not be,' said Yahweh" (v. 3). The verb literally means, "to have compassion," "to pity," "to grieve," or "to feel repentance." Amos's intercession is successful. Here is a striking testimony to the power of intercession.

7:4-7. Second vision: a shower of fire averted. In the second vision, Amos witnesses God's calling down a judgment of fire upon both "the great deep" and the land above. The "great deep" refers to the primal waters beneath the earth (see Gen 7:11, Ps 36:6). Fire has played a significant role previously in Amos as in chapters 1–2, which refer to the destruction of invading armies. Perhaps the fire here represents some military threat to Israel that is viewed symbolically as the potential return to primeval chaos. In similar fashion to the first vision, Amos quickly responds, "O Lord GOD (*Adonai Elohim*), cease, I beg you! How can Jacob stand? He is so small!" As previously, Yahweh relents: "This also shall not be."

7:7-9. Third vision: a wall built with a plumb line. Rather than visions of destruction, Amos is now shown an everyday scene: a wall built with a plumb line. This is no ordinary construction site, however. Yahweh acts as the construction foreman overseeing the quality of the work. It is "Yahweh" who stands by this wall built with a plumb line. Amos is asked to describe what he sees. His response is simple and straightforward and reflects the glance of the layperson. "A plumb line" is all he sees. Yahweh, however, sees more. Like the inspector at a construction site, Yahweh sees a wall out of plumb. The wall does not measure up.

"See, I am setting a plumb line in the midst of my people Israel." Just as this is no ordinary inspector, this is no ordinary wall. The construction under scrutiny is nothing less than the people of God. Unfortunately the people of God do not measure up. When a wall is out of plumb, it must be torn down. It may not be safe or structurally sound. It certainly may not live up to its purpose. Like the out-of-plumb wall, Israel will be destroyed.

Here we encounter the harshest words in all of scripture.

I will never again pass them by; the high places of Isaac shall be made desolate, and the sanctuaries of Israel shall be laid waste, and I will rise against the house of Jeroboam with the sword.

Places of worship where one might expect to encounter joy, song, dance, fellowship, and God's presence will become desolate places. The divine judgment will even extend to the house of Jeroboam, the royal household. No one and no thing is left out. Sadly, there is no prophetic intercession here. The time for that is past. Amos stands silent. Israel does not measure up. There is nothing left for the prophet to say in Israel's defense. Foreshadowing the horrible and final words of the fourth and last vision, Amos offers no response—"Be silent!" (8:3).

Theological Grist

In the visions of Amos 7 we see another side of Amos. Amos the fiery prophet of judgment is also an intercessor for the people of Israel. Amos is called to deliver harsh words in a smooth season. His message is unpopular, as the narrative of 7:10-17 clearly reveals. The prophets are sometimes viewed as conspirators and traitors (see, for example, Jer 37:1–44:30). Nevertheless, Amos can feel the weight of judgment upon Israel, and he asks God to relent.

The message he is called to proclaim and the burden of ministry he is called to bear are not easy. Amos is concerned about the people he is called to prophesy to by God. The prophet is a testimony to the power of intercession. Like Abraham and Moses before, Amos even seeks to restrain God, thus becoming an intercessor for the people he must bring difficult words to. He becomes their advocate (cf. 1 John 2:1).

Yet, just as there is an end to all restraint, so there is a point beyond which even intercession is a viable option. Israel has reached that point. The journey of life often provides numerous points for turning back, turning around, beginning again. But it is possible to go past the point of return. It is possible to make choices that bring finality—with respect to relationships, trust, health, and life itself.

Israel reached that point of no return. Throughout its history the nation has shown a propensity to view relationship with God as a privilege rather than as a responsibility. This is always a temptation for the people of God. Israel reaches a point when the only words left to be spoken, as difficult as they are, are "never again"—the most difficult words ever spoken. "I will never again pass them by." Choices in life matter. They make a difference. They have lasting impact upon our futures. Some choices lead to "never again"—a painful reality.

Application for Preaching and Teaching

"Never Again"
Amos 7:7-9; Romans 8:31-39

"Never again," John said. "Never again will I trust you. I can't forgive you this time." Ann could feel the pain in his words. His heart was broken, and now he was going to break hers. "Never again! No more chances! How could you do this again? How could you show so little respect for our marriage, our family, your children, me? It's over! Never again. I refuse to live like this any longer." There was a finality in his words she had never heard before. After a long series of indiscretions, she had finally added the straw to break the proverbial camel's back. She did not blame him. In fact, she felt pained by his pain. She really did love him. Or was it just the comfort of the relationship she loved— the respectability, the home, the children, their status in the community?

She had *done it* this time, and she fully knew it. She could tell it in his voice. She had hurt him before, and he had responded with harsh words, but never like this. They had always come back together—eventually. Never had she heard, "never again." She shuddered at the thought of it, the implications of his verdict. It sounded so final. She had gone too far this time. Stunned, his words kept echoing though her mind: "never again, never again, never again!" "How could it have reached this point?" she asked. Her failure was a burden she would bear for the rest of her life.

Bob's shock was beyond belief. The words hit him like nothing had ever hit him before. His breath was taken away. He had to grab hold of the wall to hold himself up. He felt as though he would pass out. "You have AIDS." A deep numbness set in. "Did the doctor say what I thought he said? Surely this is a dream. Wake me up from this nightmare!" Even though it was Bob's worst nightmare, it was no dream. It was reality. He had always felt compassion for those who caught the disease through no fault of their own. He had even had pity on those who caught it because of their actions. But never did he think he would hear those words concerning himself. "You have AIDS."

As he walked to his car, shivering in disbelief, he realized that he could not remember another word the doctor said. All he could remember were those three words that he would remember every day for the rest of his life. Never again would there be a day, however long he lived, when these words would not haunt him and overshadow everything he did. Never again would he awake to a carefree day with a full life to enjoy, no worry, full of hope. Never again. All because of a stupid, careless act.

He knew there was no one else to blame. The choice had been his. He had been careless one too many times. He had allowed himself to become infected. He had known the risks and yet exposed himself to the disease—unprotected. He alone was responsible. He would live with the consequences of his actions for the rest of his life, now to be much less than it might have been. Never again a carefree day to bask in the sun, to enjoy family and friends, to plan for the future, without the horrible reality that is AIDS. Never again.

The sirens were so loud he thought his ears would burst. "What in the world happened?" Todd asked himself. As he shook his head, in a feeble attempt to focus his eyes and to remove the fog from his head, he realized for the first time that he was in trouble. He recognized the men who were walking around the two cars as the highway patrol. He heard the sound of the ambulance as it grew closer and closer to the scene of the accident. There were too many lights flashing and too much noise. His body was numb. "How am I going to get out of this?" he continuously asked himself as his mind raced over and over the events of the last hour.

Already the men had attempted to ask him questions. Strangely, he found that he could not answer. He wasn't sure whether it was the effects of the accident—the shock of it all—or the drugs that he had taken only an hour ago. There didn't seem to be anything physically wrong. He was shaken up, but there were no broken bones, no blood. He had actually been pretty lucky. As the men walked toward the car once more, they began assisting Todd to his legs. "Can you walk over to the ambulance?" the attendant asked. "I think so," Todd said as they helped him to his feet. Leaning upon their shoulders, he began the short walk from the wreckage of the cars to the back of the ambulance. Briefly surveying the damage to both cars, he began to realize just how lucky he really was.

It wasn't until he saw the other car that his mind cleared enough to remember the driver of the other vehicle. As they walked, he could see two paramedics working with a woman stretched upon the ground. There was blood. She had not been so lucky. They walked right by the woman and the paramedics, so close he could have reached out to touch them, so close he could hear their conversation. "Hurry with that IV. I think we're losing her. Her BP is bad. Wait, I lost her pulse. Hurry. Lets start CPR!" "O my God!" Todd thought. "Why is this happening? And it's my fault. O, my God, why did I take those drugs? What have I done? O God please save her. I promise, never again. I will never do it again. O God please do something! What have I done? Never again. God help me. I will never do it again!"

If we were to make a list of painful words, surely among the most difficult, painful, hurtful words in human language would be the words "never again." "I will never trust you again. Never again will I consider you a friend. You will never work for this company again. Never again will you be welcome by this family. I will never talk to you again as long as I live." We could add dozens of other possibilities to my list.

"Never again." These words are almost always painful. They sound so final—as if there is no going back. No more chances. When "never again" is spoken, we know something has gone too far. The time for change has passed. Forgiveness disappears as an option. It is all over. There is nothing we can do except live or die with the pain and the consequences.

Sometimes life goes on after never again. Perhaps most of the time it does. Sometimes, however, what comes before never again means that life will not go on, or that it will be severely limited. In any case, never again usually leaves a burden to bear, a pain in the deepest recesses of the heart, a sense of brokenness and failure—scars to wear and bear for the rest of our lives. "Never again" are difficult words to hear, and they leave their marks upon us, impacting who and what we are as well as all that our future holds.

Amos of Tekoa, like many prophets before and after him, received a call to deliver harsh words in a smooth season. It is interesting to discover the different reactions to the prophetic call. Some prophets offered excuses such as the one Jeremiah did: "Ah, Lord God! Truly I did not know how to speak, for I am only a boy" (Jer 1:6). God promised Jeremiah to put words in his mouth, though he was very clear about the direction his ministry would take. "Today I appoint you over nations and over kingdoms, to pluck up and to pull down, to destroy and to overthrow, to build and to plant" (1:10).

The prophets are often stereotyped as spokespersons of "gloom and doom." Words of judgment are considered the singular subject of their preaching. While it is generally true that prophetic preaching in the Old Testament more often than not brought words of judgment from God and calls to repentance, it would not be fair to say that the prophets particularly enjoyed this aspect of their ministry.

Amos, whose recorded preaching is as full of words of judgment as any prophet, is portrayed in the seventh chapter as one who interceded with God on behalf of Israel. The prophetic ministry of intercession is significant. Chapter 7 records that Amos witnessed two visions of judgment (7:1-3, 4-6). In the first he witnesses a locust plague devouring the land just after its crops have begun to sprout forth from the ground. In the second vision Amos sees a firestorm devouring the land. Both the locusts and fire are clearly presented as actions of the Lord God. Yet, in both cases, Amos offers the following intercession: "O Lord God, forgive, I beg you! How can Jacob stand? He is so small!" Amos's petition is followed by Yahweh's response. "The LORD relented concerning this; 'It shall not be,' said the LORD."

This is a comfortable picture, isn't it? It is nice to know that the word of judgment is carried out by one who is able to restrain the severity of the judgment. It makes us feel good when we consider the possible impact of intercession. Amos was able to restrain God's judgment. As Lord Tennyson wrote, "More things are wrought by prayer than this world dreams of" *(Idylls of the King)*. James tells us that "the prayer of the righteous is powerful and effective" (5:16). Haven't we all benefited from the power of prayer? Though we do not fully understand its power or significance, or why it sometimes seems effective and sometimes not, we continue offering our intercessory prayers as individuals and as communities of faith because we are quite sure that it can make a difference.

Yet there is another, perhaps more difficult, side to this coin. The portraits of Amos restraining God are followed immediately by a scene in which Amos remains silent (7:7-9; cf. 8:1-3). In the third scene, as in the previous two, God "shows" Amos something. This time, however, it is not a picture of judgment, but a scene out of everyday life. Amos sees a wall and "the Lord" standing by it with a plumb line in his hand. Amos is asked a simple question: "What do you see?" Yet Amos's vision is impaired. He only sees a wall and plumb line. God, however, like an inspecting architect, sees a wall built improperly, a wall out of line, a wall that should be torn down. It is so bad it must be rebuilt from scratch. More significantly, that wall is Israel. "See, I am setting a plumb line in the midst of my people Israel." "See, Amos, see. Can't you see what a mess my people are in?"

The words that follow are difficult. They are horrible words, yet words that reveal a truth about life that we dare not miss.

> I will never again pass them by; the high places of Isaac shall be made desolate, and the sanctuaries of Israel shall be laid waste, and I will rise against the house of Jeroboam with the sword. (7:8b-9)

Never again. The time for restraint is past. The time for intercession is past. Amos is silent. Never again. High places for the worship of God are to become desolate. The sanctuaries are to be laid waste. Interestingly, the places of worship are singled out in this vision of judgment. The house of Jeroboam, or the court, also does not escape. Important symbols of both government and religion are to be destroyed by God. Never again. No more chances. It is over. Never again. The prophet is speechless, silent. No more time for intercession; only silence remains.

I don't know about you, but I am uncomfortable with the "never again" of Amos 7. It's not what I want to hear. It's not what I expect to hear. Don't we usually think of God as one in whom there is infinite love, in whom there are more chances for forgiveness than we have opportunities to fail? Surely we are more comfortable with the words of Jeremiah when he reports God to say of his people, "I will forgive their iniquity, and remember their sin no more" (Jer 31:34b). We are more comfortable with Psalm 103:12, which comforts us with the words, "As far as the east is from the west, so far he removes our transgressions from us." And when we reach the New Testament, we find comfort in the good news of the gospel that though "the wages of sin is death, the free gift of God is eternal life in Christ Jesus our Lord" (Rom 6:23). We celebrate the fact that ultimately nothing "will be able to separate us from the love of God in Christ Jesus our Lord" (Rom 8:39b).

As a Christian I am big on grace and small on "no more chances." I don't like never again, especially when it comes from the lips of God. The sweeping picture of grace that is painted across the pages of the New Testament makes "never again" extremely uncomfortable. Surely, however, life teaches us, and Amos is teaching us, that this portrait of God's grace that we so readily accept does have a flip-side. I am convinced with Paul that "nothing shall separate us from the love of God in Christ Jesus our Lord." Yet there are things from which even God's love will not spare us. We may trust in God's power to forgive, but too often forgiveness still leaves behind the scars.

Perhaps in our praying we should follow the advice of Saint Ignatius of Loyola who said, "Pray as if everything depended on God, and act as if everything depended on oneself." You see, we have choices to make in this life. We will not get through life without making many decisions with serious implications for ourselves and others. In our youth we sometimes find ourselves feeling as if we are invincible. There is nothing a teacher, a parent, a friend, cannot fix. We mess up but rarely suffer lasting damage. There is usually a mother, father, or grandparent to embrace us. Perhaps too we discover the embrace of God.

With the coming of the teenage and young-adult years, however, the choices become more complicated and numerous. Sure signs of maturity are feelings of complexity and of being overwhelmed before the decisions we must make. Whom will we choose as friends? How will we perform in school? What career path do we take? Do we embrace integrity and character? Do we choose a healthy lifestyle? How do we treat our neighbors? These and hundreds of additional complicated decisions come before us on the pilgrimage of life, and each demands a response—sometimes on a daily basis. We dare not miss the point that our responses are crucial for our lives and for the lives of others.

Amos interceded for his people. He could even restrain the anger of God. Yet there came a time when Israel's decisions brought the nation to a reality that even God could not prevent. Our choices in life impact our lives and the lives of others. I fully believe that nothing can separate us from the love of God, but you and I also know that we can be forgiven and yet still have the scars. We can make decisions that set actions into motion that neither we, nor even God, can prevent.

Israel went too far. Its decisions and actions were sins against God, but they also impacted the very future of the nation. We too make decisions each day that have within them the power to change lives, our own and others. Sometimes decisions lead to pain, destruction, and even death. God's power to forgive is not in question, but neither is our power as free agents in God's creation to choose wrongly and find ourselves hearing those words that we really never want to hear: "Never again!"

Chapter Nine

A Kept Minister

Amos 7:10-17

Allen Walworth

Background

Context

The conflict between Amos, the "seer," and Amaziah, the priest, recorded in Amos 7:10-17 occurs in the text immediately after the third of five visions that come to Amos. The oracles of the prophet are collected in the first six chapters of the book, followed by these five visions (7:1–9:6). The presentation of the visions with their adjacent narratives is significant. A progressive pattern emerges:

Vision of the Locusts (7:1)
> intercession by the prophet (7:2)
> Yahweh relents from carrying out the destruction (7:3)

Vision of the Fire (7:4)
> intercession by the prophet (7:5)
> Yahweh relents from carrying out the destruction (7:6)

Vision of the Plumb Line (7:7-9)
> conflict between Amaziah and Amos (7:10-17)

Vision of the Summer Fruit (8:1-3)
> sayings that reinforce finality of judgment (8:4-14)

> Vision of Yahweh beside the Altar (9:1-4)
> doxology of Yahweh's power to destroy (9:5-6)

The structure in the textual presentation of these visions reveals some progression toward narrative climax. Each vision foretells judgment and destruction for Israel, but after each of the first two visions Amos intercedes for the people, resulting in a change of Yahweh's mind. The reader might expect such an intercession again after the narrative of the third vision (the plumb line, 7:7-9), but here the pattern of judgment/intercession/Yahweh's relenting is broken. Instead of the prophet's intercession, the text inserts the episode of Amaziah's rebuke to Amos. It is as if to say that Israel is beyond intercession now—they do not have a prayer! In fact, the very ones responsible for holding the plumb line of God's precepts before the people, the priests, are the ones who now persecute the prophets.

This conflict illustrates and confirms the third vision. There is no relenting on the part of Israel or Yahweh. Consequently, the remaining visions are merely reinforced by the interspersed narrative verses. The fourth vision, which follows the passage of this exegesis, pronounces "the end has come upon my people Israel; I will never again pass by them" (8:2). The cycle of visions closes with unrelenting doom and destruction upon Israel as judgment for its sins, until the entire section concludes with one of Amos's doxologies.

The reader of Amos has already seen the book's pattern for inserting concluding doxologies after sections of judgment in 4:13 and 5:8. Perhaps this allows narrative and emotional "breathing room" after such harsh words of judgment. The doxologies also serve final punctuation to the oracles or visions by reminding the hearer/reader that Yahweh has the power to create (4:13), to use the creation for blessing or destruction (5:8), and to destroy the entire creation if Yahweh so chooses (9:5-6). The freedom and power of Yahweh to be God is the final chorus of Amos's use of doxology.

Amaziah and Amos

Outside this passage, we know very little about Amaziah. From Amos 7:10-17 we know that he was a priest serving in the temple at Bethel.

We can only speculate what station Amaziah might have held within the hierarchy of priests serving that prestigious site. The Hebrew text of 7:10 does not use a definite article with his position (hence he is identified as "a priest of Bethel," rather than as "the priest of Bethel," contrary to the translations of NRSV, RSV, NIV, and KJV).

We may infer that Amaziah served as a high priest at that sanctuary, or that he had some other personal or professional relation to the king, since he was the one who took initiative to report the sayings of Amos to Jeroboam II, and he seemed to feel empowered to speak for the king and the Northern Kingdom, as well as for the sanctuary at Bethel. Beyond these inferences we know nothing of his station. We know only of his priesthood and assignment at the sanctuary where the royal family worshiped.

To serve as priest in this temple was no insignificant post. We know that Bethel had been a sanctuary of special note for Israel ever since patriarch Jacob/Israel slept there and had a vision of his own, receiving God's blessing and promise (Gen 28:10-22). During the monarchy, Bethel (meaning "house of God") became one of the primary shrines of worship for the Northern Kingdom, the southern counterpoint for the sanctuary at Dan in the North. These two places of worship rivaled the Solomonic temple in Jerusalem after the division of the monarchy under Jeroboam I and Rehoboam in 722 B.C.

Jeroboam I set up the alternate sites of worship for the Northern Kingdom and established a priesthood from the laity (1 Kgs 12:26-33) to consolidate the new splintered nation around its own cultus. Two centuries later, under Jeroboam II, the system was still in place. Needless to say, there was considerable enmity between the cults of North and South, between Bethel and Jerusalem. The bitter competition between the holy sites of North and South provides part of the backdrop for the confrontation between Amos, prophet from the South, and Amaziah, priest from the North.

Amos the prophet is the only person so named in the Hebrew Bible (not to be confused with Amoz, the father of another great eighth-century prophet from the Southern Kingdom, Isaiah). His name means "one who carries a load." Indeed, he did! The message of Amos was a load to bear for the prophet and a heavy load to bear for the people of Israel.

The occupation of Amos has stirred some debate among scholars. With only Amos 1:1 and 7:10-15 to provide details, a number of salient facts are unclear or unknown. Amos was not a simple poor shepherd, but perhaps a more prominent sheep rancher or government official. If so, it is all the more remarkable that Amos could so clearly identify with the injustices endured by the poor and be so scathing in his denunciation of the rich! But history has known other sons and daughters who were born with silver spoons in their mouths, yet who used those spoons to feed others (for example, Francis of Assisi).

Perhaps Amos became a wealthy man through his shepherding business, but he never forgot a more humble origin. One might even speculate that a wealthy Amos was able to finance his own living while an itinerant southern prophet speaking in the North. We cannot know for certain, but the traditional depiction of Amos as a poor shepherd-turned-preacher may not be true. The preacher or teacher of this text might justifiably wrestle (or playfully imagine) with the other possible readings of Amos's social status.

In 7:14-15 we have the only other clue to the occupation and background of Amos. In his reply to Amaziah, Amos refutes the implication that he is a "professional" prophet (Amaziah accused Amos of preaching for bread and urged him to do so back in his hometown—an interesting irony to which we shall return soon). The Hebrew text reads:

> Not a prophet, I, and not a son of a prophet, I, but a herdsman, I, and a tender of sycamore trees. And the Lord took me from following behind the flock and the Lord said to me, "Go, prophesy to my people Israel."

Notice that the Hebrew text does not supply the connecting verb in 7:14, a convention that the English translator must supply. Perhaps Amos is saying that he used to be a layperson, a shepherd and tree-dresser, before God called him to his current role as prophet. This reading, which is implied by the past tense verbs supplied by KJV and NIV ("I was no prophet . . . but I was a herdsman and dresser of sycamore trees"), assumes that Amos now sees himself as a prophet due to the Lord's call, but not because of any particular training in a guild of prophets, often called "sons of the prophets" (cf. 1 Kgs 20:35; 2 Kgs 2:3-4; 4:1, 38). Indeed, this interpretation fits the life experience of many women and men whom God has called from the ranks of other professions to the ranks of ministry. But the reader will beware of reading his or her own life story into that of Amos.

It is also a plausible reading of Amos 7:14 to supply present tense verbs, as chosen by NRSV and RSV ("I am no prophet . . . but I am a herdsman and a dresser of sycamore trees"). Under this reading, Amos is responding to Amaziah's rebuke with even more forceful denial of the trappings that often attached themselves to prophetic office. Here Amos is contending that he is no professional religious spokesperson (an epitaph that fits Amaziah much better), but is still a layperson. Like Stephen and Philip of Acts 7–8, Amos speaks and acts totally by the direct command of God, but he still sees himself as a shepherd and tree-dresser by profession. He does not preach for his bread.

Either reading underscores the importance of the direct call of God on Amos's life and words. Amos will not take orders, nor edit his message, nor change his venue by the authority of priests or kings. He obeys a higher authority. Like Martin Luther King, Jr. or Mahatma Ghandi, he practices civil disobedience. Like Daniel before Nebuchadnezzar or Peter and John before the Sanhedrin, Amos "must obey God rather than men."

Amos's self-description as "a herdsman and a dresser of sycamore trees" in 7:14 helps illuminate his background, but does not completely resolve all of our questions. The word used for herdsman, *boqer*, is *hapax legomena* (a word used only this once in the Hebrew Bible), and is therefore difficult to translate with certainty. Some scholars have wondered if this unusual word might be a scribal misreading for the typical word for shepherd.[1] Others have noted that *boqer* may be derived from the term for cattle (*bakar*).

Could it be that Amos may have raised more than one type of livestock, both sheep and cattle? A "dresser of sycamore trees" refers either to the practice of pinching the unripe bitter figs that grow in clusters from the stems of the plant (in order to promote ripening) or to the practice of opening the clusters to allow insects trapped in the fruit to escape, thus promoting proper ripening.[2] In either case, these were menial tasks and may suggest again a more modest social status for Amos.

One other difficulty arises from this brief autobiographical statement of Amos. The sycamore fig, which is part of the mulberry family of trees, grows only in altitudes below 1,000 feet above sea level, such as the Jordan valley and Egypt. Recall that Tekoa is 2,500 feet above sea level. Perhaps Amos farmed sycamore figs not too many miles east from Tekoa toward the Jordan valley. Does this suggest that Amos was a wealthy farmer with business interests in a number of locales? Or that he was a poor, migrant farmer, with experience as a shepherd and as a fig-pincher who had to find work wherever he could? Again, the interpreter has the opportunity and responsibility to weigh the evidence.

The Rebuke of Amaziah

Amaziah accused Amos of treason against Jeroboam II, "Amos has conspired against you in the midst of the house of Israel." Perhaps his accusation also includes the personal insult that this southern seer has done so in the very heart of the Northern Kingdom. Although the recorded words of Amos do not include the exact wording of Amaziah's quote, he is not wide off the mark. Amos 7:9 contains a clear reference to a sword against the house of Jeroboam, and Amos has repeatedly prophesied the captivity of the nation in exile (4:2-3; 5:5, 27; 6:7; 9:4), a national fate that usually inferred the death of the current king. Of course, Amaziah is incorrect in a critical way regarding Amos and his message. Amos is not declaring this word by his own authority, but by the Lord's. Amos would say that the sins of the king and the people have conspired against Jeroboam, or even that the Lord has conspired against him. The message burns, so Amaziah wants to burn the messenger.

We do not know what response, if any, Amaziah received from Jeroboam. His further remarks to Amos may be the king's command, or they may be Amaziah's own counsel. At any rate, Amaziah urges Amos to flee back to Judah (7:12). This territorial solution to the "Amos problem" reminds one of Pilate's attempt to send Jesus to Herod upon hearing of his Galilean origins. This suggestion may be Amaziah's attempt to save the life of Amos from the king's wrath, or a concession to the people's growing respect for the prophet, or a sign that he lacked authority to physically arrest Amos. Removing the annoying messenger seemed the simplest way to remove the annoying message. This priest of Bethel did not become assigned to such a politically sensitive post without some skill at handling difficult situations in diplomatic and politically correct ways. Surely Jeroboam would commend Amaziah for his quiet but forceful removal of the problem prophet!

The command to Amos to "eat your bread there, and prophesy there" (7:12) stands in clear contrast to his restriction from Bethel, the "king's sanctuary." The implication is that Amos should preach for a living, for his bread, back home in Judah. Such a mercenary supposition of the motivation for Amos's preaching stung Amos and earned the retort of 7:14-15.

The Reply of Amos

The prophet answers the priest with swift and spirited defense (7:14-17). Amos contends that his call to prophesy at all, and its locus in Israel, came by direct command from the Lord. His authority and courage came from the same source. Amos did not derive his authority from the prophetic guild (a son of the prophets), nor from prophetic training and income (he is a layman, a herdsman, and a fig grower). Consequently, Amos cannot respect the authority that Amaziah represents in his prohibition, the authority of king and priest. Like Peter and the other apostles before the Sanhedrin, he "must obey God rather than men" (Acts 4 and 5).

The direct prophecy against the house of Amaziah is unique in the recorded words of Amos. It is the only prophetic word addressed directly to an individual or family in the book. Its form is similar to other prophetic oracles ("Hear the word of the LORD"), but picks up on the command of Amaziah to silence Amos. Amaziah is told that his land will be taken (should a priest own land, according to Levitical custom?), and his family humiliated, and he will die in an unclean land (a particularly loathsome site for death for one committed to ritual purity).

The point of this clash between Amaziah and Amos is over the issue of power and authority. Who is allowed to speak in the name of the Lord? Who speaks the true spirit of the Lord? Whose authority will prevail in the ordering of historical events? Will the power of the priest, enhanced by a prestigious station assignment and backed by royal governmental authority, govern the events of the day? Or will a lone voice prevail from an unwelcome foreigner, a prophet with no credentials other than his sense of call?

The Amaziahs of the world usually win the battles for the microphone, the podium, the news "sound bites," and the board room. But every once in a great while, a tiny cry turns the world and topples the towers of Babel. Eight centuries before Christ, that cry was offered by Amos. In Christ, that cry began in a manger and concluded on a cross. And since Christ, that cry has been whispered in dungeons and shouted over flames many times. Who will take up the cry next?

Application for Preaching and Teaching

A Kept Minister
Amos 7:10-17

It happens slowly. An almost imperceptible drift toward the rocks, undetected until the minister's spiritual keel is snagged upon the reef. It is the subtle slide from the free space of prophetic vision to the entangled web of purchased blindness. It is the process by which a lion's roar is muted to a gentle whimper by the seduction of power and security. Another would-be prophet has become a kept preacher. How does it happen?

A young pastor preaches with passion and freedom. Soon her reputation spreads throughout the town. "Come hear our new preacher," they said. "She's got power in the pulpit." And they came. And they applauded her rhetoric, wept and laughed with her illustrations, and greeted her at the door of the sanctuary each Sunday saying, "Let's see you top that one!" After a short while, the pressure to perform made each Sunday seem like the Super Bowl to the young pastor. She gestured and joked her way through many sermons, learning which homiletic buttons to push in her congregation to ring the amen bell.

Soon she became an expert at reading her people's interests, but lost her expertise at reading the Bible and finding her people's needs. Like an insecure politician, she became an avid follower of the current congregational opinion polls and failed to become the leader she was called and gifted by God to be. In a word, she gained the whole town, but she lost her prophetic soul. She had become a kept minister.

He had been the minister of music for a number of years at a small church. One day a wealthy member of the choir asked if he would have the choir sing a patriotic anthem she composed. He listened to the words and music and was frankly unable to find any way to use the "gift" of this anthem in the music ministry of the church, but the woman was one of the very few wealthy members of the church. His own music budget depended in large part upon her designated gifts to the choir library, so he gave in and used the anthem she composed on July 4th Sunday.

The next week, he opened his mail to find a check for $1,000—an expression of her thanks for his decision. Each successive year she approached him with the same request, and each year the envelope arrived with the $1,000. No one else knew about the monetary gift, and, quite frankly, he needed the money to supplement his salary. Each year he seemed to need that extra income to get through the summer. Although he felt cheapened by the practice, and although he cringed at the thought of doing that anthem each year, he could not find a way to refuse the annual request. He had become a kept minister.

Another minister served a church in a city where the primary employment was military bases and defense contracts. When the war broke out, it signaled an economic boom for that city. The minister had some concerns about the war and whether the motives of the government were as altruistic and national-security oriented as presented by the White House. But the entire town was whipped into a frenzy of national patriotism and personal economic hope over the current international crisis.

The mayor asked this minister to address the annual citywide prayer breakfast. The subject was the war. His church leaders felt the invitation was an honor for both the church and the minister. A number of them suggested biblical passages and illustrations he might use to support the war effort. "This will be your finest hour of ministry in our city," they said, beaming with pride.

As the minister approached the podium at the prayer breakfast, he looked into the expectant faces of a thousand citizens, many of them leading citizens from his own congregation. He thought of his own concern and outrage over certain aspects of the war, but he also thought of his family's happiness in the city, his mortgage, and the good reputation he enjoyed in the community. He swallowed hard, opened his mouth, and blessed the war with eloquence, baptizing the conflict with the language of faith. The people cheered. And in the distance, a cock crowed twice. He had become a kept minister.

And Amaziah? How did it happen with him? He served as a priest, perhaps with unusual distinction. He became known for his diplomacy, his loyalty, his ability to smooth rough situations—his ability to keep the peace. The reward for such loyalty and such ability? A call to service in the sanctuary at Bethel, the temple where the royal family often worshiped. Amaziah had hit the big league. His career was a success. He was finally serving "big First Church." He had the attention of King Jeroboam. He was priest at the national cathedral.

Such a position exacts a cost, however. He was to be spiritual guardian of the status quo. He was to offer the official blessing of the national and royal platform. It was not hard to bless either, for the days of Jeroboam were days of great prosperity for those closest to the king. Surely God must be blessing if the coffers are overflowing, the budget is met, and the pews are full! It was a happy time to be at the top of the economic ladder. And the longer Amaziah ate at the king's table, the more he developed a taste for the king's cuisine. All he had to do was curry the king's favor, to stay in the royal delight.

Everything was fine, until the visitor from Judah arrived with a blistering message of judgment for Israel's sins. He only said what most people already knew: The poor were being oppressed in these days of economic prosperity, justice was denied the powerless and penniless, and those who worshiped in the Temple at Bethel with exact liturgical precision could still harbor a heart that was far from God. Like the little boy in the fable who dared to say that the emperor had no clothes, Amos merely said out loud what many others (including Amaziah in his secret heart of hearts?) knew to be true. He reminded them that God was none too pleased. When Amos preached about the Day of the Lord and announced to Israel "Prepare to meet your God," it did not sound like a happy encounter. But it did have the ring of truth.

Amaziah was thrust into a crisis of decision regarding the preaching of Amos. The prophet had attacked the "powers that be" for their active or passive role in creating and propagating an unjust society under the banner of religion and nation. Amaziah, who was part of that web of power, fought back. His counterattack was a play for reinforcement from the king, twisting the words of the prophet to political sedition rather than moral rebuke (reminds one of the accusations by another set of priests concerning Jesus before Pilate). Further, Amaziah called into question Amos's motivation for preaching (that he simply spoke for bread, a hired gun of sorts), focused on the prophet's foreign status and brief tenure in the North, and banished him from the king's temple. Amaziah attacked everything except the prophet's message itself. Like a defense attorney with no real case, Amaziah could only take cheap shots at the witness, hoping to intimidate Amos. The evidence itself confirmed Amos's testimony. Amaziah's efforts merely became an illustration of that very prophetic word. The plumb line of the priesthood was crooked.

The path is a dangerous one that merges political/economic power with religious leadership, when profit and prophet walk too close. Without appropriate distance, prophetic insight becomes astigmatized. Ask Billy Graham about the risks of being too close to the president. Ask southern preachers who defended slavery from the pulpits in the nineteenth century or segregation from the pulpits in the twentieth century. When the minister places the knees under the linen tablecloth in the master's house for Sunday dinner, it is difficult to see, much less condemn, the social injustices upon which that table sits. But must ministry be defined only by antagonism? Is the prophet's only message one of fire and brimstone? No, not at all. Listen to the doxologies of Amos. Listen to his words of hope and calls for repentance.

The minister or church that would keep its prophetic voice does not have to sacrifice its pastoral or priestly voice. Much that pretends to be prophetic preaching these days is merely thinly veiled anger anyway.

Before launching a missle named "prophetic preaching," the minister will do well to check for compassion in his/her heart, and for clarity of God's commission to choose this particular target. Are the stakes high enough? "Not every battle is Armageddon," as Ernest Campbell used to say. The wise minister, the effective church, listens to the winds of the Spirit and chooses carefully and compassionately those times when the Spirit blows against the prevailing wind of the culture. The sadness is that for so many of us, when that time comes, we do not even have our sails ready.

If the church is to discern the wind from the Wind, it must spend its energy looking for ways to please God, to serve God, to worship God. The church must say its prayers, read the Bible, be self-critical, and keep an ear to the edge of the circle, for that is usually where corrective change is initiated. An unkept church is not withdrawn from the world, nor is it disengaged from the powers-that-be. But that church keeps it eyes and heart open when patriotism and religion seem to be indistinguishable, when salutes to flags and hymns to God seem synonymous, when the words "God" and "country" fit too nicely in one sentence.

Kings and countries need a prophetic voice that is not purchased, whose text is not "spin-doctored." Several decades before the confrontation between Amos and Amaziah, King Jehoshaphat of Judah and King Ahab of Israel were preparing for war. As they sought spiritual counsel, Ahab produced 400 staff prophets who all predicted complete victory for their employers. Jehoshaphat had been a king long enough to distrust the sound of his own company's public relations, so he insisted on a second outside opinion.

Only the prophet Micaiah was left free of the king's payroll and protection, and only Micaiah heard the hard truth from God that the battle was ill-fated. The announcement of that truth landed the prophet in prison, but at least he was still more free in spirit than the 400 purchased prophets (1 Kgs 22). Whenever power has tried to fetter a free prophet, that voice carries even farther (for example, John the Baptist, Paul and Silas, Peter and John, John of Patmos, Martin Luther King, Jr., Nelson Mandela). A free nation needs a free church, even when and because that relationship is strained at times.

And the prophets like Amos, from whence do they come? They are blown by the Spirit into the moment of prophecy, often from the edges of the religious community—in the case of Amos, a man with little professional training but a great deal of life experience. Perhaps he was even a wealthy man, a merchant with multiple business pursuits and wide travels. But if so, his wealth did not dull his senses to hear the outcry of the poor, and his origin in Tekoa did not make him take a spectator's role in Bethel. What comes over persons so that they see with such clarity and speak with such boldness? As Amos himself said, nothing other than a sense of the call of God. "The lion has roared; who will not fear? The Lord has spoken; who can but prophesy?" (3:8).

Diogenes, the philosopher, dined only on lentils, lived in a humble manner, and yet offered keen insights of wisdom. One day Diogenes was approached by a fellow philosopher, Laertes, who ate well at the king's table. Said Laertes to Diogenes, "If you would learn to cultivate the king, you would not have to eat lentils." Diogenes replied, "Laertes, if you would learn to eat lentils, you would not have to curry the king."

Would you be an Amos or an Amaziah? Pass the lentils, please.

Notes

[1]See *Interpreter's Bible*, vol. 6 (New York: Abingdon, 1956) 836; and *Broadman Bible Commentary*, vol. 7 (Nashville: Broadman, 1972) 129.

[2]Page Kelley, *The Book of Amos* (Grand Rapids MI: Baker Books, 1966) 21.

Chapter Ten

Amos
A Word for Our Times

Amos 8

Sheri Adams

Background

The summer fruit vision follows the visions of the locust, fire, and the plumb line. In commenting on our text, Ralph L. Smith[1] suggests that this vision took place in the following way: It is late summer. The harvest has been gathered. The people are feeling good—their needs for the winter have been taken care of, and they are expecting another good harvest in the year to come. They have come to the Temple in Bethel to celebrate the good harvest, the New Year, the expectation of the fall rains, and another good harvest. Smith suggests that perhaps part of the ceremony included the appearance of a priest to offer up the basket of fruit and invoke God's blessings for the year ahead. The commentary writers agree that the people interpreted their good harvest, good fortune, and material blessings as a sign of God's favor.

At this point in the ceremony, instead of the professional, "status quo" prophet, Amos appears. Sure enough, Amos has another word from God. The word for "end" in Hebrew, Smith says, is a wordplay or a pun on the word for summer fruit. In effect, through Amos God is saying, "You planned on enjoying your summer produce, but I am planning your destruction as a nation." There will be no harvest next year, and no New Year's celebration. The end has come. Note that Amos does not call the people to repentance. It is too late—even for that.

In verses 4-6, Amos returns to his theme of social justice. The poor of the nation are suffering miserably, and Amos lays most of the blame at the feet of greedy merchants. Elsewhere in the Old Testament, the text speaks of people who lie awake in their beds plotting evil. Here we see folks "enduring" religious observances when they would much rather have spent the day doing what they did best: cheating people.

Smith says they put false bottoms in their baskets and, in that way, made the "ephah small." Although the law prohibited having two sizes of weights, one for buying and one for selling, these dishonest merchants were guilty of breaking the law dealing with just and honest measurements (see Deut 25:13-16; Lev 19:35-36). They would have two sizes of the shekel, which was the standard measure for weighing and selling gold and silver nuggets and bars. The larger shekel was used for selling, so the merchants would receive more of the buyer's gold or silver. The smaller shekel was used for buying, so they would part with less of their own gold and silver. They also cheated the people in that they sold them shoddy or worthless merchandise—the "sweepings of the wheat," for example.

In verse 9, Amos turns to what the Lord will do about the dishonesty—and the establishment of a Better Business Bureau was not God's solution. Amos gives a new interpretation to the Day of the Lord. The popular expectation was that the Day of the Lord would be a time when God would bring about the defeat of Israel's enemies.[2] This, of course, would have meant even greater prosperity for Israel. Already interpreting prosperity as a sign of God's blessing, the defeat of its enemies and the resulting prosperity could only mean that God was really pleased with the nation.

Amos was quick to destroy such a false interpretation of the Day of the Lord. Instead of military conquest and victory, it will be a day of military defeat. Instead of the wealthy continuing to trample the poor in increasing prosperity, they will be trampled by their enemies and brought to ruin. Instead of a victory day of joyous celebration, the day will be more like an earthquake, a day of terror. Instead of living out their lives in wealth and comfort, the people will live in poverty and mourning, in sackcloth and baldness. According to a custom of the time, one would shave a part of the head as a sign of mourning. This mourning was also to be like the grief for the loss of an only son. This phrase is significant because in Israel the family name was passed down through the sons. Should the only son die without an heir, the family's hope for the future died with him. Amos's mourning may also be understood to be saying that Israel has no hope for the future.

Worst of all, the Israelites will experience the all-too-human emotion of being unable to find God in their hour of darkest need (vv. 11-12). Israel would learn the hard way what we can only hope that we never have to learn: the only thing worse than God's judgment is God's absence. Israel had to learn that a nation or an individual can endure anything with God present to comfort, guide, and bless. Without God's presence, nothing can fill the void—not wealth, nor comfort, nor privilege.

Amos pictures a situation so bad that even the young and strong cannot endure (v. 13). What hope is there, then, for the old and weak and sick? We often say or read that the strength or the future of our nation is in our children. While we should never neglect or mistreat children, the future strength of a nation or a family does not ultimately depend on its children, but rather on its relationship to God.

Many questions are raised when one attempts to interpret verse 14. Commentators generally ask, what is the relation of this verse to the preceding ones? What is the meaning of Ashimah of Samaria or "the guilt of Samaria"? What does "as the way of Beersheba" mean? Was this verse written by Amos, or was it a later interpolation by a writer protesting the situation in Samaria after its resettlement by the Assyrians who established their own cults there (2 Kgs 17:29-33)?

We cannot determine who is said to be swearing in verse 14. It could be the young men and women of verse 13. It could be the people traveling the earth in search of a word from God. It could be the dishonest merchants. It could be the people brought in to live in the land after the Israelites have been taken into exile. Whoever they are, they are involved in idolatry. It is known that "Ashimah," a goddess, was worshiped in Samaria by the men of Hamath (2 Kgs 17:30). The passage could also be referring to the golden calves that were set up at Bethel and Dan and were worshiped by the people of Israel.

According to Smith, the text indicates that these gods were false gods. They appear in connection with the Hebrew word, *he*, which tells the reader that the oath is being made to a false god. The Hebrew word, *ha*, is used when the oath is being made to Yahweh. So these names and phrases almost surely indicate that these are false gods, and that idolatry is at the core of Israel's troubles. This interpretation is certainly that of the other Old Testament prophets.

J. D. Smart emphasizes this departure from God in his article on Amos in *The Interpreter's Dictionary* of the Bible.

> The heart of Amos's faith was the conviction that only a nation in which the dealings of men with one another are just can be in any true sense a people in covenant with God. For him it was axiomatic that the whole future for Israel depended upon its relationship with God. Divorced from God, the nation must quickly perish. Therefore, the dishonesty of judges, the cruelty of rapacious businessmen and landowners, and the irresponsibility of prophets were not merely blemishes upon the national life, to be exposed and reformed; they were evidences of a deeper and more serious sickness, the repudiation of its God by the nation, and thus a betrayal of the nation that must bring its ruin. It is the justice, holiness, and purity of God that calls for justice, holiness, and purity in the common life of Israel.[3]

Application for Preaching and Teaching

Amos: A Word for Our Times
Amos 8

If ever there was a book of the Bible that is pertinent for our times, it is Amos. An important part of the background of the book is the growing gap between the rich and the poor of Israel. One would have to be totally ignorant of the political and social situation in the U.S. at the present not to realize that many people believe the growing gap between the rich and the poor is one of the major problems facing us as a nation.

An article in the April 17, 1995 issue of the *Fort Worth Star-Telegram* began with this headline: "Economic gap grows: Egalitarian society a myth, studies show." The article read:

> New studies on the growing concentration of U.S. wealth and income challenge a cherished part of the country's self-image: Rather than being an egalitarian society, the United States has become the most economically stratified of industrial nations. Even class societies like Britain, which inherited large differences in income and wealth going back to feudal times, now have greater economic equality than the United States, according to economic and statistical research.

One source quoted concluded, "We are the most unequal industrialized country in terms of income and wealth, and we're growing more unequal faster than the other industrialized countries."

According to this article, Federal Reserve figures from 1989 show that the wealthiest 1 percent of U.S. households, with net worths of at least $2.3 million each, owns nearly 40 percent of the nation's wealth. The top 20 percent of Americans, households with a net worth of $180,000 or more, own more than 80 percent of the country's wealth, a higher figure than any other industrial nation.

The article related how both "liberals" and "conservatives" react to the information. Liberal social scientists worry about poor people's shrinking share of the nation's resources and the consequences in terms of economic performance and social tension. Margaret Weir, a senior fellow in government studies at the Brookings Institution, called the higher concentration of incomes and wealth "quite divisive," especially in a country where the political system requires so much campaign money. "It tilts the political system toward those who have more resources," said Weir, adding that financial extremes also undermine the "sense of community and commonality of purpose."

Conservatives express skepticism about the statistics and their significance. Marvin Kosters, an economist at the American Enterprise Institute in Washington, said he believes the wealth gap, as measured, is being used as a false villain. "I think we have important sociological problems," he said, "but I don't think this gets at it all that well."

Murray Weidenbaum, professor of economics at Washington University in St. Louis and chairman of the Council of Economic Advisers under President Ronald Reagan in 1981–1982, said the measures tend to overstate the gap by overlooking government programs such as food stamps and Medicaid. Nevertheless, he said he is uncomfortable with greater concentration of wealth "unless there's a rapid turnover in which this year's losers will be next year's winners."

It would be interesting to know whether or not the people of Amos's day debated the issue as we do. Is it a good or bad thing for the country to have inequality between rich and poor? Is it important? What does it mean? As we read Amos, and indeed all of the prophets, we can know the answers they would give if they were here. The gap between rich and poor is a problem for a country. It is not just a sociological, economic, and political problem; it is a moral and spiritual problem.

There is one vast difference between our country and the one in which Amos lived. At one time in Israel's history, all of the people had entered into a covenant with God in which they had promised to keep God's laws. We Christians are the spiritual descendants of the ones who made those promises. Some of God's laws were intended to provide safeguards to prevent the gap between rich and poor.

Several years ago I spoke to a meeting of North American missionaries in South America on the subject, "Evangelism at Risk: The Dangers of Ignoring the Biblical Teaching on Poverty and Wealth." On that occasion I remarked that one of the most interesting and revealing parts of Old Testament law is the concept of the Jubilee and all that it implied. Here we find economic justice from God's point of view.

Most of the Jubilee concepts are spelled out in Leviticus 25, although Jubilee ethics and theology lie behind many of the Old Testament passages. Probably the most distinguishing feature of the Jubilee was the concept of a tribe's land as an eternal possession. Land, like people, could be bought and sold, but only for fifty years at a time. Leviticus 25:23 reads: "The land shall be sold in perpetuity, for the land is mine; with me you are but aliens and tenants." Verses 25-28 deal with the person who has become poor and has sold some or all of his or her property: "What was sold shall remain with the purchaser until the year of Jubilee; it shall be released in the Jubilee, and the property shall be returned" (v. 28).

Other aspects of the law dealing with Jubilee included the canceling of debts and the freeing of slaves (also done every seven years) and a double Sabbath for the land, which meant no agricultural work to speak of for the people for two years. No wonder they were told to proclaim liberty throughout the land (25:10)! The obvious result is that, although a family might fall on hard times and become poor, it could never permanently lose the means to support itself. Every fifty years, the family would get another chance.

The flip side, of course, is that every fifty years the rich were more or less back to square one. Under this system, getting rich was not impossible, but it was not easy. Exploiting the poor was not impossible, but there was a limit to how long the same people could be exploited. To make things even more difficult for the rich, they were prohibited by God from ever charging interest on money lent. Many scholars believe that the ancient Jews never actually practiced the Jubilee. They must have practiced it at least partially, however. Otherwise, it does not seem logical that the Bible would contain condemnations of the abuses of it.

This is the background against which we read the book of Amos. Amos is talking to people whose ancestors promised before God to follow God's laws, laws that included actions that would have, if practiced, closed the gap between rich and poor. Not only did they not follow God's law concerning Jubilee, they also broke other laws of God. We see this in the text. God commanded merchants to be honest in their business dealings. Instead they were cheating people in every way possible. They had baskets with false bottoms. They had one weight for buying and another for selling, and the advantage was always in the merchant's favor. They sold garbage—"the sweepings of the wheat" (8:6b)—to the poor.

They bought "the poor for silver and the needy for a pair of sandals." This is a powerful statement. It stays with us and tempts us to condemn them. But how many of the poor of our country are locked out (trampled on, brought to ruin, as the text puts it) for want of a telephone to receive a call from a prospective employer, or want of transportation to a job interview or a job, or want of the proper clothes to wear to an interview. Many times it is easier to tell ourselves that they do not want to do better than it is to admit that we have not done all we can to help.

Why is it that the rich in the day of Amos seem wicked, while we, who almost surely have more of life's comforts and material resources than they did, do not? Both groups, they and we, are religious, if by religious we mean that we are going through all the right motions. But what both they and we have done is ignore the commands of God concerning the poor.

Annie Dillard has put this so succinctly in her autobiography, *An American Childhood.* She grew up in wealth and privilege, the daughter of an insurance tycoon. Of her home, she wrote, "These houses seldom changed hands. The next step up was the right hand of God." Of her church experience she said,

> The adult members of society adverted to the Bible unreasonably often. . . . Why did they spread this scandalous document before our eyes? If they had read it, I thought, they would have hid it. They didn't recognize the vivid danger that we would, through repeated exposure, catch a case of its wild opposition to their world. Instead they bade us study great chunks of it, and think about those chunks, and commit them to memory, and ignore them.[4]

This we have in common with the rich to whom Amos spoke: We have ignored the parts of God's commandments that would threaten our levels of comfort and security. It is much easier and safer to believe as they almost surely did that our material well-being is a sign of God's blessing. The text reminds us of the dangers of ignoring God's word:

> The time is surely coming, says the LORD GOD, when I will send a famine on the land; not a famine of bread, or a thirst for water, but of hearing the words of the LORD. They shall wander from sea to sea, and from north to east; they shall run to and fro, seeking the word of the LORD, but they shall not find it. (8:11-12)

I am sure that Christians of all ages have felt that their times were in special need of a hearing of God's word. It certainly seems to be true of our time. The Bible has been used to scold us, shame us, and scare the socks off us; yet few of us are really familiar with the Bible. We need to read it, all of it, lots of times. We need to allow God to do God's life-changing work as we read and study and seek to know God through our reading of the Bible. We need to read it alone; we need to read it in groups. When we do, we will acquire the vision and courage of Amos, and we will be able to speak the truth of God to our generation as he did to his. We will see that God's judgment is not a given. We can receive God's blessing instead, but it will be on God's terms, not ours. Treating the poor as God would have them treated is still part of the terms of the covenant.

Notes

[1] Ralph L. Smith, "Amos," *Broadman Bible Commentary*, vol. 7 (Nashville: Broadman, 1972) 81-141.

[2] J. D. Smart, "Amos," *The Interpreter's Dictionary of the Bible*, vol. 1 (New York/Nashville: Abingdon, 1962) 120.

[3] Ibid, 121.

[4] Annie Dillard, *An American Childhood* (New York: Harper & Row, 1987) 134.

Chapter Eleven

Grace beyond Judgment

Amos 9:1-15

Rex A. Mason

Background

Of all passages in the book of Amos—which is full of theological, social, and historical interest throughout—9:1-15 is one of the most interesting and most discussed. The great variety of scholarly interpretations of it is evidence of the many questions it raises. There are several ways of dividing the text as it stands but, broadly speaking, the chapter falls into two main divisions: 9:1-8a, last of five visions with oracles of judgment; and 9:8b-15, oracles of salvation. These may be further subdivided as follows:

9:1-8a
- 1-4   Last vision and threat of total annihilation
- 5-6   Hymn-like doxology (the third in the book, cf. 4:13; 5:8-9)
- 7-8a Rejection of Israel's specal covenant status

9:8b-15
- 8b   Exception to total judgment for "the house of Jacob"
- 9-10 Limitation of judgment to "the sinners of my people"
- 11-12 Promise of restoration of the house of David
- 13-15 Promise of paradisical fertility and security in the future

Clearly, one of the main issues to be decided is just how these two very different parts of the chapter fit together.

9:1-4. This is the last of the five "visions" that are narrated in the book of Amos (cf. 7:1-3, 4-6, 7-9; 8:1-3). After the first two visions, Amos responds by interceding with God for the people, but each of the other visions is accompanied by oracles showing the religious and theological significance of what Amos sees. The form of this final vision differs from that of the others, which said that God "showed" Amos some incident or event and involved Amos in the explanatory process. Here Amos just sees the Lord standing "beside" (or even "on") the altar and hears God's words.

This difference in form has led some scholars to suggest that this is a later "vision" added to the others by an editor. Prophets could vary the form they used in portraying a series of visions or events (cf. Zechariah's seven visions in Zech 1–8), however, and Amos varies the formula of his sayings against the nations in chapters 1 and 2. More likely, this form is to emphasize the direct and immediate action of Yahweh against the sanctuary, and thus to provide a sinister climax to the whole process described in the visions.

It is not clear just whom Yahweh is addressing with the command to strike the pillars of the sanctuary and bring it down on the heads of persons in the congregation. Some scholars have seen this as a call to the prophet to engage in an act of "prophetic symbolism," while others have pointed out that it would have been difficult for a human being to reach so high and so wide! Some have seen this as a call to Yahweh's angelic messengers who formed the "council of heaven," while others have seen it as more general, impersonal construction in the call for the pillars to be shattered.

Clearly, it is Yahweh's action, whoever may be the instrument, and we must not miss the terrible sense of sacrilege this would conjure up for the faithful at Bethel. (The sanctuary is not specified, but since Amos spoke so much against the northern sanctuary of Bethel, it is often taken that it must be meant here. On the other hand, the lack of specific reference may be intentional. "The sanctuary" could be any place or symbol of the nation's official religious life).

If we translate the Hebrew "I saw the LORD standing on the altar," then we have an allusion to the people's faith that Yahweh dwells in the sanctuary (cf. Ps 132:13-18) and that the divine presence guarantees blessing and protection (cf. Ps 46; 48). But, as Amos keeps doing, the assurance is inverted. Yahweh is there alright, not to protect them but to judge them.

An important treatment of Amos by Hans M. Barstad has shown that Amos by no means confined himself to the social and political sins of the community. He strongly attacked the religious sins as well in the same way that Hosea did. Thus the final vision, centering on the sanctuary as it does, constitutes a particularly fitting climax to his whole message.

The totality of the judgment is stressed in the threat of 1b, that, if any persons survive the collapse of the sanctuary, they will all be slain by Yahweh's sword. Even if some survive to go into captivity, even there they will be killed (v. 4). Indeed, there is a cruel inversion of a later promise to those very exiles in Jeremiah 29:11: "I know the plans I have for you, says the LORD, plans for your welfare and not for harm."

Another passage also receives an ironic inversion here, namely Psalm 139:7-12. It speaks of God's care for each individual from which none can ever escape. Amos speaks in almost the same words of the impossibility of any individual escaping the judgment of God. It is impossible to say which passage was written first but, taken together, they show the double aspect of God's presence and power. God may be known in either judgment or mercy. Thus, 9:1-4 forms a strong climax to the whole series of the visions.

9:5-6. Whether the three doxologies were original to Amos or, as some have suggested, added later when his words were read and used liturgically, there can be no doubt of their appropriateness at this juncture. The God who threatens this judgment is the creator of all the earth and the heavens and has power to carry out all divine purposes. With its possible allusions to the judgment of the Egyptians at the Reed Sea and the flood of Genesis 6–9, the doxology, as the German commentator Rudolph has said, "stills all protest or appeal or hope of escape."

9:7-8a. This passage is characteristic of Amos's method of shocking his hearers. Amos takes the very cardinal basis of their faith, God's redemption of their fathers from Egypt with its corollary that God has chosen them for a special covenant relationship and given them the land of Canaan for their special inheritance, and he turns it against them. He did it in 3:2, where he allowed this special election of Israel by God, but turned it against them by saying that special privilege meant special responsibility, Here, he claims, while their faith is true, it is nothing that by itself automaticallly guarantees lasting immunity, for God has been involved in the movements of all peoples.

By likening his hearers to the Ethiopians, Amos mentions a people known to inhabit the very edges of the then-known world (Homer refers to them as "the farthest outposts of mankind"), and they were often thought of and treated as servants (cf. 2 Sam 18:21; Jer 38:7). By mentioning the Egyptians and the Syrians, Amos takes two people from whom Israel had always thought themselves distinct and from whom God had preserved them when they threatened Israelite occupation of the promised land. Understood like this, 9:7-8a does not contradict 3:2, but warns that there is no such thing as "unconditional salvation history."[2]

9:8b. At this point, real difficulties for interpretation begin. After the utter totality of judgment just threatened, how can we make sense of this saving clause? Even syntactically it appears to be an afterthought, introduced by the phrase "except that" and overloading the parallelism of the first two lines of the verse. What logical sense does it make? Wellhausen's famous phrase still sums up the problem when he described verses 8-15 in their relation to the earlier part of the book as "roses and lavender instead of blood and iron."

For these and similar reasons, many commentators have therefore taken verses 8b-15 to belong to a later stage of the book's development, when, during or after the exile, Amos's words were seen to have been fulfilled in what befell Judah as well as Israel. Yet, at the same time, those who survived the exile were seen in terms of a "remnant," spared by God and returned to their homeland in order to experience the future blessing of which the prophets were also thought to have spoken.

That such later readings of the prophetic words took place and have left marks on the books as we now have them seems indubitable. Indeed, it would be strange if later generations had not found that the earlier words of God also applied to their new situation and taken them to heart accordingly. It is difficult to know otherwise why they should have preserved the prophetic collections. It seems clear, for example, that there has been a Judaean editing of the book at some stage (1:1, 2; 2:4-5). Not all recent commentators (Rudolph is a notable instance) have accepted that the whole of 9:8b-15 is later than Amos, however, and some argue as to which can be adduced for their originality (even if now in a somewhat altered form).

Some commentators point out that Amos does once or twice seem to imply at least the possibility of the survival of some kind of "remnant" (3:12; 5:4-6, 14-15—though they really cannot be used to support a remnant doctrine). Apart from that, Amos's attacks are, for the most part, against the leaders in society—the rich, the priests, judges, and rulers—and they are attacked for their oppression of "the righteous poor" (2:6-8; 4:1; 5:11-12; 8:4-6, and others).

What, then, did Amos think would be the ultimate fate of those "righteous poor"? Although he does not go into it, surely he would have seen it as most unjust of God if they were to be punished twice, first by their wealthy and oppressive overlords, and then by God. Further, the terms Amos uses to describe "the poor" (Hebrew *dal* and *'ebyin*) are exactly the terms used in those psalms of lament in which "the poor" cry out to Yahweh for justice against the oppression of their rich and powerful overlords. Those psalms make it clear that they will not cry to God in vain. Of course, we can never be sure of the date of any particular psalm, yet it would stretch credulity to say that such prayers formed no part whatever of the worship of pre-exilic Israel.

If, then, the worship of the sanctuary brought its assurances that God would rescue and preserve the faithful poor, it would be strange indeed if this had left no impression on the prophets, and that they neither shared nor expressed any such faith. Further, we have to ask just what is implied by the use of the phrase, "house of Jacob." We can dismiss any idea that this might mean God would save Judah as over against the northern kingdom of Israel. Nowhere does Amos ever echo the Deuteronomic idea that worship in the North was sinful because it was held away from the only true sanctuary of Jerusalem. He attacks the worship of the North because it was a cloak for injustice and was not matched by obedience to God's laws, not because of its location. Amos has just predicted the downfall of "the sinful kingdom" (v. 8a), which suggests the whole organized state with its center in palace and temple. So closely were these connected in the theocratic kingdom that the same Hebrew word stands for both.

Notice that when Amaziah tells Amos to leave, it is because his words against the sanctuaries of the North (8:9) are seen as sedition against the royal house (8:10-13). Possibly, then, the contrast of "the house of Jacob" with the "kingdom" in 9:8 means that it stands for the true community of faithful Israel, whether found in Israel or Judah—those who were the true heirs of their father Jacob—or as Paul calls faithful members of the Christian church the true sons of Abraham (Rom 4:11-12). In 3:13 the kingdom is identified in accusation with "the house of Jacob," but this, of course, is their own claim. Other instances in the prophetic collections suggest that, in God's future, the true "house of Jacob" will survive (Obad 17; Micah 4:2). Certainty is beyond us here, but we should not deny the sentiment of verses 8b-15 to Amos too quickly.

9:9-10. The picture of the sieve suggests a process by which all the rubbish falls out to the ground, but what is valuable is preserved. This is the only place in the book of Amos where such a specific distinction between sinners and others is made but, for the reasons stated above, that does not mean Amos could not have made it. Note that the "sinners" are still "the sinners of my people." This is wholly consistent with Amos's view that belonging to the people of God did not guarantee automatic immunity. Because they are God's people but have ignored the responsibilities this special status involved, they will suffer judgment (cf. 6:1).

9:11-12. This is, perhaps, the strangest oracle to conceive of as coming from the lips of Amos. Since most of his ministry was in Israel, the fate of the house of David would have meant little to his hearers. They had long since rejected it. Further, it seems to suggest that the house of David has fallen, while the reference to Edom also suggests a time during or after the Babylonian exile. The literature of that time breathes a great deal of hostility toward Edom for its alleged treachery when Judah was under threat. The term used, "booth of David," is the same term used in Isaiah 1:8, where Zion is pictured as just somehow hanging on in a time of great peril like a harvester's booth in a field. That has led some scholars to suggest a time before the exile when Jerusalem was threatened but did not succumb, which could have been in Amos's lifetime.

On the other hand, "breaches" and "ruins" suggest something fairly complete, and there is no record in the Old Testament of such a devastation of Jerusalem before the sixth century. It clearly suggests a restoration of the Davidic royal line and of the full extent of the former Davidic empire, including "Edom" and "all the nations who are called by my name," probably those surrounding peoples who were brought under subjection to David (including Israel). Clearly, such a promise, even if spoken by Amos, would have gained added force for those persons who returned from exile in Babylon, and we know from Haggai that there were hopes of the restoration of David's line (2:21, where the terms "servant" and "signet ring" are used of Zerubbabel, but elsewhere are used of the Davidic king).

As we have suggested, it is a tribute to the power of God's word to go on speaking that later generations could take earlier prophetic words and find new application of them to their own circumstances. One cannot ignore the warning implicit in this oracle as well as the promise, however. Only on the other side of the destruction of the present "kingdom" does any hope of restoration as an act of divine grace lie.

9:13-15. The picture of the future age of salvation is of miraculous fertility of the land (the words probably mean there will be two harvests in the year). They fulfill the old covenant promises, especially in Leviticus 26:5 and Deuteronomy 28:1-6. Amos's words appear to be quoted almost exactly in Joel 3:18. They will know peace and security so that cities and towns can be rebuilt with confidence (v. 14), and they will never again be driven away into exile (v. 13). All this revolves around God's act of "turning," the Hebrew word having overtones not only of a "turn" of fortune, but of a "turning" to Yahweh in penitence and trust. This is just what they had failed to do in response to Yahweh's earlier dealings with them (4:6, 8-11)—"yet you did not return (same Hebrew word) to me." Thus, all the threats that Amos had predicted (3:11, 15; 4:2-3; 5:11, and so on) will be reversed by the same sovereign action of God in grace that God had manifested before in judgment.

Application for Preaching and Teaching

Grace beyond Judgment
Amos 9:1-15

Judgment Begins at the House of God

It is difficult for us to recover the sense of blasphemy and sacrilege that God's words must have conveyed to the prophet and his listeners. The sanctuary, and everything in it, was sacred, just because people believed that God dwelt there and was to be encountered there. The old story of Uzzah in 2 Samuel 6:6-11 brings this home. Almost involuntarily he reached out a hand to steady the sacred ark on its journey to Jerusalem, and he was struck dead. To the psalmist, the entrance of pagans into the temple and their ravaging of its buildings was an act of unbelievable sacrilege (Ps 79:1). It was the place where God dwelled: "This is my resting place forever; . . . I have desired it" (Ps 132:14), while the presence of God in the sanctuary guaranteed the people immunity from all assaults: "God is in the midst of the city; it shall not be moved" (Ps 46:5).

The vision granted to Amos in this chapter and God's words to him do not deny the presence of God in the sanctuary in the least, but God's presence is a two-edged sword. For those who trust God and are obedient to the Word, the divine presence is all that is meant by *shalîm*. To those who defy God, however, God's presence is "a devouring fire." Those who congregate in the sacred precincts are not immune. Indeed, as Amos has shown throughout, judgment begins at the "house of God." Those who have had privileged revelation of God, who have been graciously called by God to be God's people and who have known God's protecting and guiding hand, are summoned to special responsibilities. Their disregard of the divine is a specially heinous crime.

Of course, in the days of ancient Israel, the sanctuary and the palace were inextricably connected (the same Hebrew word means both "temple" and "palace"). It is difficult for those who live in lands where the separation of church and state is either guaranteed by constitution or an accepted matter of everyday practice to realize what this meant. The king was seen to rule by the choice and sanction of God and to exercise rule in God's name (see Ps 132:11-12; 2 Sam 7:16). He chose his courtiers and officials and ruled through them. The worship in the sanctuary was under the sanction of the king and guaranteed his power, so that the priests were official members of the "establishment."

Because of the combined governmetal and priestly powers, prophets such as Amos often attacked kings, rulers, and priests. Therefore, Amos's attacks on the worship at sanctuaries such as Bethel, cloaking as it did abuse of their God-given powers by the "establishment figures" in their oppression of the poor, could be construed as sedition by the chief priest, Amaziah (7:10-13). It was all a cruel caricature of the realization expressed in the temple worship that the well-being of the whole community depended on the king's right relationship with God and his true exercise of justice in the name of God (Ps 72:1-4).

Can any of this be preached meaningfully today when the political and social realities are so different? We who live in democracies are not so helplessly dependent on "what our betters do to us." We cannot simply shrug off all the blame on to our leaders and "betters." Indeed, we have in our own hands, by the exercise of democratic rights, control of the kind of leaders we get. We share responsibiity with them. Amos's kind of preaching must surely seem at least somewhat patronizing, if not downright irrelevant, to our societies come of age.

Perhaps two things may be said here. Even in democracies, those persons who are entrusted with leadership at any level exercise influence on others, for good or ill. If I am entrusted with any kind of special position, I am faced with special responsibility. If I am a teacher, which interests me more: my own research and career, or the well-being and development of my students? If I hold political power, am I more concerned with the perks that go with it and advancement up the ladder of ambition, or in using my position to do some good for the more vulnerable members of society? If I am in business or commerce, during any crisis of conscience, will I keep quiet in order not to rock the boat and be branded as a "whistle-blower" or "troublemaker," or will I speak out against corruption? If I am a "career churchperson," am I getting lost in the whole bureaucratic process of keeping the institution alive, or am I uttering a prophetic voice that keeps calling the church back to its task of serving and witnessing to the world? Position does give us influence; special position brings special responsibility. Amos tells us that each of us is judged accordingly.

Recently the British press has been deluged with "sleaze" stories involving policiticans, people in high social places, and even some church people. Some of this is due to sensationalist, circulation-grabbing newspaper reporting. Most often, the alleged crimes have not been enormous. Yet, taken together, accompanied by stories of marital unfaithfulness in high places, they both reflect and help to create a "snouts-in-the-trough" atmosphere of greed, where any principle can be sacrificed in the pursuit of wealth or power or instant gratification. Even in our modern, democratic societies, special privilege does bring special responsibility.

Amos tells us something else. We all help to create the moral environment of our society. However great or small we are, however important or insignificant our position, we have influence beyond ourselves. We help to create a heaven or a hell for those around us. We encourage a few to goodness and faith, or we make doubt and cynicism easier. We may think of it this way.

There are some artesian wells, especially in parts of India, that are connected deep underground to common water tables. If one farmer cares for his well and keep its waters pure and sweet, he improves the water of his neighbors. If he allows it to become contaminated and brackish by neglect or malice, he damages the health of others. That is a great biblical principle. No individual can keep the consequences of his or her own sin to himself or herself, just as persons cannot keep the influences of their own love and faith to themselves. We are all "bound together in the bundle of life" (slightly to mistranslate 1 Sam 25:29).

We do not really need psychiatrists to tell us that, as parents, we are already influencing our children from even before their birth. This is the heart of the Christian doctrine of "original sin," and it expresses the real truth behind the words "the sins of the fathers are visited upon the children to the third and fourth generation." An amusing sticker reads: "We are spending our kids' inheritance." The fact is that, morally and spiritually, we are all either forging or squandering our kids' inheritance. Amos's words of warning and judgment have disconcerting relevance for us all, not just for today's equivalents of kings, rulers, and priests.

Amos's words of judgment against the sanctuary have other contemporary implications. This picture of God, or God's agent, striking the pillars of the sanctuary to bring it down on the heads of the worshipers is only the climax of a whole series of denunciations of their religious worship and organized cult life. "I hate, I despise your festivals . . ." (5:21); and "Take away from me the noise of your songs . . ." (5:23) are typical examples, but elsewhere also he can equate worship at Bethel and Gilgal with "transgression" (4:4-5).

We cannot dull this by saying that Amos shared the view of Deuteronomy that only worship offered at Jerusalem was legitimate, since nowhere does he show any awareness of or concern with such a view. (In any event, think of Isaiah who criticized the worship at Jerusalem in terms very close to those of Amos, for example Isa 1:10-17.) So this all raises the question: Did the prophets think that organized, sanctuary worship with all its sacrifices and special festivals was evil in itself, or was it that God rejected the worship of these people because they had corrupted it? Had it become a cloak of respectability for their evil lives, a substitute for, rather than an expression of, their true love for God?

Most scholars today take the latter view, although the first was popular in the days when Protestant scholars tended to find convenient a supposed Old Testament rejection of Catholic ritual and stress on sacraments. For example, in the Isaiah passage alluded to above, Isaiah denounces their "prayers": "Even though you make many prayers, I will not listen" (1:15). Isaiah was not against prayer as such, but God would not hear these worshipers' prayers because "your hands are full of blood."

This raises important issues for the attitudes we take to church structures today, the whole of the organized, denominational systems that we have reared, some of them taking on almost the characteristics of large business corporations and all of them demanding large expenditures of money and person-power to house them, administer them, and maintain their structures. The communities involved in them face larger and larger demands on their time on committees and fund-raising activities, all to support their evermore complex life and ever-growing number of departments and organizations. All this can lead to increasingly introverted self-absorption, in which the church, from being only a means to an end, comes dangerously close to being an end in itself, no longer serving and witnessing to the world with a cutting edge.

Any administrative body faces the danger of favoring conformity over radical dissent, and so the whole thing becomes more and more "conformed to this world and its structures." It is rather like a notice board I once saw: "Do not throw stones at this notice board." When, like the sanctuaries of northern Israel of old, the church becomes an end in itsef—its sanctity invested in its own life, structures, and worship—it usurps the place of God. Sooner or later, it needs to hear the cry that Amos heard from God: "Smite the capitals until the thresholds shake, and shatter them on the heads of all the people."

When institutions and structures drift toward divinity, they may take various possible lines of action. In effect, some people may say, "To blazes with the structures. Let us have done with the institutional, organized churches and break away from them." Such a voice has been increasingly heard in Britain with the rapid growth of various forms of the movement for charismatic renewal, and it has led to the forming of house groups, some of which own no denominational allegiance. It seems attractive, but the chase for "structure-free" relgion is an elusive one.

Back in the 1960s, when a radical tide of secular discontent was sweeping through many of the British churches, I once saw an advertisement in a religious journal that ran: "Will all those interested in forming the Non-Church please write to . . . " No doubt, so many persons replied that before long an office had to be hired, a secretary employed, and an annual assembly of all like-minded Non-Church members arranged!

No joint human activity can run without structures, and there are dangers if we pretend we do not have any. The chances are the ones we do in fact have will be bad ones, but, because we do not acknowledge them and constantly bring them out to subject them to God's judgment, they will end by taking over, just like the old ones. The Old Testament presents us with a sterner challenge not to repudiate the structures, but to keep them constantly under the searching judgment of God. It implies never becoming so wedded to them that we can never scrap them or change them. It means refusing to invest them with quasi-divine authority. It means constantly asking whether they are still serving the purposes for which they were set up. It means that God's vested interest in structures always takes priority over ours. It will recognize that the rushing torrent of God's spirit will often seek out fresh channels by which to flow into this parched world.

Everything human is provisional. This is the greater challenge, the challenge of both Old and New Testaments. We are constantly commanded to ensure that our church structures are the servants and channels of the Spirit, not the amassed silt that is now clogging the water of life. The Old Testament contains both the assurance that the temple, with its means of grace, is appointed of God as a valid meeting point between God and God's people. Yet, the Old Testament contains also the constant prophetic challenge to that temple, which the people of every age need to continue hearing.

Grace beyond Judgment

The most remarkable thing about this extraordinary ninth chapter in Amos is the complete switch of mood and content between its first part, verses 1-8a, and its second part, verses 8b-15. We have seen that this has led many commentators to deny the later part to Amos, seeing it as the "softening" work of a later hand to take account of the remarkable change of fortune for those who had returned to Palestine from exile in Babylon. We offered some arguments to suggest that this need by no means be necessarily so.

Actually, whoever the author was does not matter all that much. This is what the chapter says to us now. It brings the assuring word of God, by whichever agent that word came. Judgment is not God's last word; God's final word is of grace. Human sin can thwart God's purposes temporarily, but, in the end, God's purposes of grace and salvation will prevail. This is the tesimony of the prophetic books, of the Old Testament as a whole, of the New Testament as well as the Old. The very completeness of the break in chapter nine, the totality of the alteration in mood, is testimony to the fact that grace is entirely the work of God. Grace is not the result of human merit, not even, in the last resort, of human repentance, but of the sheer, sovereign grace of God.

But we cannot stress too strongly that the grace promised here lies only on the other side of judgment for sin. The God who is present in the sanctuary at the beginning of the chapter is the God whose presence is all-powerful, a fact supported by the doxological hymn of verses 5-6. With its hint of the destruction of humankind by the Flood and God's judgment of the Egyptians at the Reed Sea, it stresses that the Creator God is all-powerful both in the divine purposes for judgment and for salvation.

When men and women are in the presence of this God, they may know God either as judge or savior. But human sin means that this revelation starts with the fact of judgment. There can be no forgiveness, no salvation, until sin has been judged and dealt with. The saving of the "pebbles" in the sieve (vv. 9-10) lies only on the other side of the "shaking of the house of Israel among all the nations" in exile. The restoration of the house of David lies only on the other side of the ruins and breaches of its walls. The amazing fertility promised in the age of salvation (vv. 13-15) is full of allusions to the very judgments of infertility and insecurity that have abounded in Amos's threats of God's judgment for sin. Reinhart Fey has finely written of this chapter:

> The preaching of Amos shows a "Yes and No of God to His people": judgment and grace, end and new beginning, destruction and building up: the first, the urgent and necessary message, the second its indispensable corrective, leaving room for the undiminishable freedom of God.[3]

The book of Amos offers little connection between these two aspects of God's purposes of grace: judgment for sin, followed by renewal and restoration of the people and land. The only hints might be found in the prophet's own intercessions for his people (7:3-6), an intercession for sinners that twice leads God to avert the danger to the sinful people. This is not followed through, however. Could there be any suggestion of some role for the "pebbles" in the sieve (9:9-10)?

These are distinguished from "the sinners of my people." Yet, apparently, they share in the general judging, sieving process. They too go into exile. They suffer the general judgment for sin, but do they have some influence, some role to play in preparing the people for God's ultimate purpose of renewal and restoration? Amos does not say, although such a role is hinted at in the view of some by a prophet of the Babylonian exile, the prophet of Isaiah 40–55, with his picture of the suffering servant who suffers judgment for the sins of others but, by virtue of his sufferings, brings them back to a saving knowledge of God (see Isa 52:13–53:12).

If this is the role of "the true Israel," then the New Testament makes it clear that it was Jesus who, alone and fully, achieved that role. At the cross God's judgment for sin fell. Only on the other side of that cross, of that judgment, could the promises of final deliverance and restoration for Israel be fulfilled. In a way, the two parts of Amos 9 meet at the cross and empty tomb of Jesus.

Perhaps one final word as to the modern relevance of Amos is needed in relation to the promise of abundant natural fertility in the age of salvation, predicted in verses 11-15. The idea of the law codes and prophets of the Old Testament that a right relationship to God will bring abundant harvests, while sin will bring judgment in the form of natural disasters, seems at first glance a strange one to our modern way of thought. It seems yet one more facet of their teaching that makes them seem so irrelevant to contemporary congregations.

Perhaps we should think again. We are all growingly aware of urgent and vital ecological pressures in our modern world. Are not most of the threats of ecological disaster related to moral and ethical issues? The greedy and thoughtless exploitation of the earth's resources is piling up problems for the future—we really are "spending our kids' inheritance." The grasping of a huge share of those resources by the few wealthy nations is at the expense of many of the poor and developing ones. We know now that the felling of a rain forest in one part of the globe will contribute to the general over-warming of the whole planet. When we pour out CO_2 emissions from our automobiles, we are, in the words of the Director of General Environment Protection in the British Department of the Environment, "in direct relation with our neighbours throughout the world at one and the same time."

It ought not to be difficult for modern congregations, then, to see the relevance of these words of Amos. A right relationship with God and a due observance of God's laws for the stewardship of the world will make a vital difference to our experience of the blessings, or the disasters, of that world. And is not this ending of the book itself a preview of a similar promise of the gospel? Does it not herald the great promise of Saint Paul: "For the creation waits with eager longing for the revealing of the children of God . . . the creation will be set free from its bondage to decay and will obtain the freedom of the glory of the children of God" (Rom 8:19, 21)?

The preaching of the Old Testament prophets, like Amos, delivers us from all narrow views of salvation as the private, inner experience of a few individuals. God's ultimate purpose is to rule in a world in which every part of life—that of individuals, families, communities, nations, politics, education, industry, and agriculture—all witness to the wholeness and fulness of that *shalîm*, which truly reflects the nature of God as it stands.

Notes

[1]Hans M. Barstad, "The Religious Polemics of Amos," *Supp. Vetus Testamentum*, 34.

[2]James Luther Mays, *Amos: A Commentary*, Old Testament Library. (Philadelphia: Westminster, 1969) 158.

[3]Reinhart Fey, *Amos und Jesafa: Abhangingkeit und Eigenstandigkeit des Jesaja* (Neukirchen-Vluyn: Neukirchener Verlag, 1963).

Biographical Notes

Sheryl (Sheri) Ann Dawson Adams is Associate Professor of Theology and Church History at the School of Divinity, Gardner-Webb University, Boiling Springs, North Carolina. Dr. Adams is a graduate of Northeast Louisiana State University, Louisiana State University, and New Orleans Baptist Theological Seminary. Prior to her current position, she served as Associate Professor of Theology at International Baptist Theological Seminary, Buenos Aires, Argentina.

Mark E. Biddle is Associate Professor of Religion, Carson-Newman College, Jefferson City, Tennessee. Dr. Biddle is a graduate of Samford University, Southern Baptist Theological Seminary, Rüschlikon Baptist Theological Seminary, and the University of Zürich. He is the author of several publications, including the forthcoming *Polyphony and Symphony: A Literary Analysis of Jeremiah 7-20,* Mercer University Press.

William (Bill) L. Coates, Jr. is pastor of First Baptist Church, Orangeburg, South Carolina. Mr. Coates is a graduate of Coker College and Southeastern Baptist Theological Seminary and is currently completing the Ph.D. in English at the University of South Carolina. A frequent speaker and preacher, he has served several South Carolina churches.

Rex A. Mason was Fellow in Old Testament and Hebrew at Regent's Park College, Oxford, and held a University Lectureship in Old Testament at the University of Oxford until his recent retirement. Dr. Mason is a graduate of the University of Oxford and the University of London. He is a frequent guest lecturer and preacher and is the author of numerous publications, including *Preaching the Tradition* (Cambridge) and *Haggai, Zechariah, and Malachi* in the Cambridge Bible Commentary Series.

James M. Pitts is Chaplain to Furman University, Greenville, South Carolina. Dr. Pitts is a graduate of Furman University, Southeastern Baptist Thelogical Seminary, and Southern Baptist Theological Seminary. He is an experienced pastoral counselor and has served in both congregational and hospital settings. Presently he serves as Chair, Board of Directors for Smyth & Helwys Publishing and authors the prayer guide for *Reflections*, a magazine of daily devotionals.

David J. Reimer is Fellow and Tutor in Hebrew and Old Testament at Regent's Park College, Oxford. Dr. Reimer is a graduate of Ontario Bible College, University of Waterloo, University of Toronto, and the University of Oxford. He is an active lay preacher and is the author *of The Oracles against Babylon in Jeremiah 50-51: "A Horror among the Nations."*

Edmon (Edd) L. Rowell, Jr. is Senior Editor for Mercer University Press. Mr. Rowell is a graduate of Howard College (now Samford University) and Southeastern Baptist Theological Seminary. Edd, an Alabama native, has served churches in several states. He is the author of various articles and books and served an an assistant editor for the *Mercer Dictionary of the Bible* and the *Mercer Commentary on the Bible*.

R. Wayne Stacy is Professor of Religious Studies, Gardner-Webb University. Dr. Stacy is a graduate of Palm Beach Atlantic College and Southern Baptist Theological Seminary. He previously served as Pastor, First Baptist Church, Raleigh, North Carolina, and as Associate Professor of New Testament Studies at Midwestern Baptist Theological Seminary. He is the author of numerous works that have appeared in various publications.

Cecil P. Staton, Jr. is Publisher of Mercer University Press and President and Publisher of Smyth & Helwys Publishing, Inc. He concurrently holds faculty status in the College of Liberal Arts of Mercer University. Dr. Staton is a graduate of Furman University, Southeastern Baptist Theological Seminary, and the University of Oxford. He is the author and editor of numerous publications, including previous volumes in this series on Isaiah and Hosea.

Allen Walworth is Pastor of Park Cities Baptist Church, Dallas, Texas. Dr. Walworth is a graduate of Samford University and Southern Baptist Theological Seminary. Previously he served churches in Alabama and Kentucky. He is a frequent guest preacher and lecturer and has published sermons and articles in various publications.